KOKOLOGY 2

More of the Game of Self-Discovery

Tadahiko Nagao and Isamu Saito

A Fireside Book
Published by Simon & Schuster
New York London Toronto Sydney

FIRESIDE
Rockefeller Center
1230 Avenue of the Americas
New York, NY 10020

Compilation and English translation copyright © 2001 by I.V.S.
Television Co., Ltd., and Yomiuri Telecasting Corporation

Originally published in Japan by Seishun Publishing Co., Ltd.,
1–12 Wakamatsu-cho, Shinjuku-ku, Tokyo, as
SOREIKE KOKOLOGY © 1998

For information about special discounts for bulk purchases,
please contact Simon & Schuster Special Sales:
1-800-456-6798 or business@simonandschuster.com.

Designed by Liane Fuji

Manufactured in the United States of America

13   15   17   19   20   18   16   14

Library of Congress Cataloging-in-Publication Data
is available.

ISBN-13: 978-0-7432-2212-9
ISBN-10:   0-7432-2212-1

THE KOKOLOGY PROJECT TEAM

WRITERS	Tadahiko Nagao and Isamu Saito
EXECUTIVE PRODUCER	Hisataka Saito
GENERAL PRODUCER	Tadahiko Nagao Takanori Ikeda
COOPERATOR	Keiko Higashiomori
ILLUSTRATOR	Makoto Ishizuki
TRANSLATOR	Douglas Sipp, Office Miyazaki, Inc.
SPECIAL THANKS TO	James C. Vines Seiichiro Shimono Hisako Miyazaki Toshihide Ochiai Takeshi Itoh Hideaki Okada
SUPERVISOR	Isamu Saito

CONTENTS

kokology \ kō kŏl' ō jē\ *n* [Japanese, *kokoro*, mind, spirit, feelings + Greek, *-logia*, the study of] **1.** A series of psychological games designed to uncover emotional and behavioral traits of the players **2.** A popular term for the interpretation of the hidden meanings of human behavior and situational responses — **kokologist** *n* — **kokological** *adj* — **kokologize** *vi*

A WORD FROM PROFESSOR SAITO

T he spread of information technology is helping to bring the world together. By exposing differences as well as uncovering similarities, global media promote mutual understanding among people of different cultural backgrounds. Of course, differences remain, but I believe that people are truly growing closer in their hearts and minds. So it has been gratifying to hear of the success of *Kokology* in the United States and across Europe. After all, Kokology is based on psychological principles that were first developed in the West, and it was originally intended to make those ideas more accessible to the general public in Japan. To see it return to its roots and meet with such widespread acceptance and popularity has strengthened my faith in the fundamentally universal nature of the human mind.

Kokology 2, like its predecessor, is intended as a tool to generate conversation and promote understanding, to help develop and deepen personal relationships, to spur the intellect and stir the imagination. But most of all, by revealing just how much we share, it shows that none of us is alone.

—ISAMU SAITO
Professor, Rissho University

INTRODUCTION TO *KOKOLOGY 2*: KOKOLOGY AND YOU

Y ou. It's a miracle that such a small word can hold such a range of meaning. Your face, name, and smile. Your body, mind, and soul. Your experiences and memories; your aspirations and your dreams. A billion attributes and inclinations constitute the unique individual summed up in those three little letters.

But despite your uniqueness, there are qualities shared by every "you" in the world. Illuminating the shared aspects of the human experience is what has made Kokology a worldwide phenomenon. Kokology is the study of you, in the broadest possible sense. Its universality has allowed a concept that began in Japan to open up new lines of communication between lovers and friends in countries around the world. The international success of Kokology speaks for the fundamental accuracy of its underlying assumption: that people want to explore the human mind and have a good time doing it.

Playing Kokology can be a little like rummaging around a dusty old attic. You may be reluctant to get started, but once the doors and windows have been opened, the air clears and the sun shines in. The experience suddenly turns into an adventure as things we thought we'd forgotten resurface in a new light.

We all have secrets locked up inside us, and we all have a desire to know and understand ourselves. But where is the person who can uncover those secrets? Who holds the key to unlocking the hidden world within? The answer, of course, is: "You."

—TAKANORI IKEDA
General Producer of *Kokology*

PLAYING THE GAME

W hen we set out to develop Kokology, our first and foremost goal was to make it fun. After all, who in their right mind would want to play a game that isn't? The basic concept was already there—our plan was to create a game where people would imagine themselves in everyday situations and unusual scenarios and respond to simple questions. The answers are interpreted from a psychological perspective and tell us something about the way that person's mind works. It's kind of like a Rorschach test that uses words instead of inkblots.

The concept was the easy part. The hard part was keeping the balance between science and fun. Professor Saito can vouch for the science; only you can be the judge of whether we've succeeded on the fun side. I'm not a psychologist myself, but I do understand enough about human nature to know that people don't like long introductions—especially not to a book of games. So I'm going to end by leaving you with a list of eight tips for making your experience with Kokology satisfying, enlightening, and fun.

Enjoy!

—TADAHIKO NAGAO

EIGHT TIPS FOR PLAYING KOKOLOGY

1. Say the first thing that pops into your head.
The games work best when you don't hesitate or agonize over your choice of words. There are no right or wrong answers, so just relax and say whatever springs to mind.

2. Play with other people if you can.
Kokology can be read alone like any other book, but it's most enjoyable, exciting, and entertaining when you play with a partner or in a group. It's a chance to have a few laughs and get to know each other better. You may find that you have more in common than you ever suspected. On the other hand, you may find you're so incompatible that it's as though you're from different planets. There's only one way to find out for sure.

3. Don't try to predict the answers.
It's natural to want to try to outsmart the quizzes or guess what their hidden meanings may be. But what are you going to learn from that?

4. Be honest with yourself.
Kokology may be only a game, but like any good game, it can teach you something about yourself if you let it. Don't be afraid to accept the truth when a minor fault or shortcoming of yours is exposed. I can sense that you're basically a good, intelligent, and likable person. You bought this book, didn't you?

5. Be prepared.

Some of the quizzes will ask you to write something down or draw a picture, so it's a good idea to have a pen or pencil and some paper handy before you start. Advanced-level Kokologists might want to try videotaping a round of games at the next office party. The expressions on people's faces when their true characters are revealed can be priceless. And the secrets they unwittingly blurt out might be worth good money, too.

6. Don't read ahead.

This goes along with the advice of not trying to guess the answers, but it's directed at the group that likes to read the last page of a mystery novel first. Why not open yourself up to a few surprises? Is it really so satisfying to be able to say, "Oh, I knew it all along"?

7. Watch people's reactions (including your own).

The interpretations to the scenarios given in this book are only a starting point for learning more about yourself and others. Sometimes it's more instructive (and entertaining) to see how someone reacts to an answer that's a bit off target than it is to read an interpretation that's right on the money.

8. Keep an open mind.

In Kokology, as in life, it's important to keep things in perspective. There are no correct answers and more than one way of reading any situation. If you're playing with friends, take the opportunity to learn from and about them. What fun would the world be if we all thought alike? Variety is the spice of life.

WHEN IS A DOOR NOT A DOOR?

It isn't every day that you have the time to take a leisurely stroll around the neighborhood: a stroll without purpose or destination, a chance to stretch the legs, let the mind wander, and get reacquainted with some old familiar sights. On your way, perhaps you'd stop in at a cozy coffee shop, explore the paths of a favorite park, or take the opportunity to do some window-shopping. Then there are those days when it's enough just to let your feet decide your course. . . .

Picture yourself on a stroll through town. The day is beautiful and you're half-lost in a daydream. You turn onto a street that you've never been down before, and as you walk you pass a beautiful house set somewhat back from the street. Pausing a moment to admire this lovely home, you notice the door is half-open. Why is the door ajar?

1. The house is being burglarized.
2. The owner forgot to close it.
3. The owner is inside, sweeping out the entranceway.

KEY TO "WHEN IS A DOOR NOT A DOOR?"

(D) oors have a twofold significance: they may be passageways, but they can be barriers as well. In particular, the front door of a house represents its first line of defense, all that stands between its inhabitants and the uncertainties of the world outside. By imagining as open a door that should normally be closed, you envision a scenario of vulnerability and exposure. On a subconscious level, the reason you imagined for the door being open is linked to the ways that you leave yourself open and expose your own weaknesses to others.

1. The house is being burglarized.

You instantly assume the worst in any situation, and this trait is nowhere more evident than when things actually do go wrong. You never get flustered in a crisis, but only because you're much too busy panicking. So the next time disaster strikes, it's important to keep a clear head and remember to take a few deep breaths first and count to ten. *Then* you can faint.

2. The owner forgot to close it.

You aren't the type to get carried away in crisis situations. On the contrary, you're so relaxed that you may not notice a crisis is occurring at all. The mistakes you make are caused more by oversight than bad intentions, but the end results for you (and the people around you) are the same.

3. The owner is inside, sweeping out the entranceway.

You may appear to be a laid-back sort, but you never let your guard down. Achieving that constant state of relaxed alertness is what has made you into the mature individual you are. Of course, you still have your human weaknesses; you just don't put them on display for all the world to see.

POSTMARKED: THE FUTURE

L ounging around the house one Saturday afternoon, you are startled out of your reverie by the doorbell. When you open the door, you're greeted by a most unusual surprise—a pair of animal messengers has come to deliver news of your life in the future! But when you open their messages, you see they contain very different predictions of what lies in store for you. One of the animals has brought a letter foretelling a life of happiness and contentment; the other prophesies only disaster and despair.

Which of the animals below brought glad tidings and which an omen of doom? (Pick a different animal for each.)

1. Tiger.
2. Dog.
3. Sheep.
4. Parrot.
5. Tortoise.

KEY TO "POSTMARKED: THE FUTURE"

F or most people, the future is greatly influenced by their selection of a mate or life partner. The animal messengers in this scenario actually correspond to your own perceptions of the kinds of people likely to bring you joy and grief. Animals are rich and complex in psychological significance, with a range of positive and negative attributes and associations. In this scenario, the animal you chose as the bearer of the message of happiness represents the type of person you perceive as an ideal spouse, while the doomsayer animal is the type you fear would drag you down into the depths.

1. Tiger.
glad tidings: You see yourself happiest with an ambitious and powerful mate, possessed of an indomitable will to rule.

gloom and doom: You dread the prospect of a vain, tyrannical partner who struts around like a lord of the jungle and growls at any mention of sharing the housework.

2. Dog.
glad tidings: Unquestioning loyalty and absolute devotion are the things you seek most in your mate.

gloom and doom: You are utterly incompatible with those who try to please everyone and fret over what others might be thinking.

3. Sheep.

glad tidings: You see the key to contentment in a warmhearted, nurturing spouse.

gloom and doom: You fear winding up stuck with a boring homebody content to spend each day grazing the same old patch of grass.

4. Parrot.

glad tidings: Nothing would suit you better than a talkative, fun-loving partner who knows how to make you laugh.

gloom and doom: No one could suit you worse than a chattering layabout with a severe allergy to work.

5. Tortoise.

glad tidings: Your match made in heaven is serious, dependable, and sure to be there in your hour of need.

gloom and doom: The prospect of a lifetime spent with a frustratingly slow-moving, slow-witted partner is your worst nightmare.

A GLAZED EXPRESSION

Arts and crafts class is almost a rite of passage in our society, a grueling test of the human spirit in which young initiates strive to force rubber cement, pipe cleaners, modeling clay, and papier-mâché to bend to their will. And few of us can claim to have managed to avoid the experience of creating an object—be it ceramic mask, napkin holder, or the obligatory ashtray—only to be confronted by an empty expanse demanding that you do something, *anything*, to decorate it.

A plain white coffee mug of your own design sits ready for the kiln and is staring at you in blank anticipation. You have chosen to use blue glaze; now, if only you could decide on the pattern. . . .

Which of the following patterns do you paint in blue on the mug?

1. Stripes.
2. Polka dots.
3. Checks.
4. Wavy lines.

KEY TO "A GLAZED EXPRESSION"

B lue is the color most deeply associated with the inner workings of the mind, from imagination to intuition to intellect. The white surface of your coffee mug provides a blank slate and gives your mind free rein to express itself in the most comfortable, natural way. In this sense, the pattern you selected reflects the structure and strengths of your mind in its approach to creativity and problem solving.

1. Stripes.

You favor a direct and clear-cut approach, making you a keen decision maker able to resolve problems and put plans into action instantly. It's only natural that people perceive you as a leader and pillar of strength in difficult times.

2. Polka dots.

Your strength lies in the adaptive, artistic nature of your mind. This may make you appear to be a little offbeat, perhaps even eccentric to some, but you make a real contribution to the world as a creator with a unique vision.

3. Checks.

You excel at mastering the demands of the everyday, but in no way does that make you average or ordinary. Few people are able to organize their lives with such quiet efficiency. And the result of your efforts is that you always seem to have the time, wealth, and compassion to share with those in need.

4. Wavy lines.

Your gift is in generating an atmosphere in which it's easy and comfortable to feel and express love. It's not that you crave attention or affection, but people just naturally feel good about taking care of and supporting you. And all that goodwill has a ripple effect, touching the lives of those around you in subtle ways. Ask the people who know and love you—the world is a better place for your being in it.

WAVE AFTER WAVE

P erhaps it's because we instinctively trace the roots of life back to the oceans, perhaps it's something hardwired deep within our brains; whatever the reason may be, the sea holds a special power over us. The tang of the salt air, the fine spray of the surf, the soft crashing of the waves—the net effect is to stimulate and soothe. Sometimes a stroll along a sandy beach can transport you much further from your everyday reality than the actual distance you walk. That may be why the sea holds a special place in lovers' hearts. It provides them with the chance to journey together, if only for a brief time, into another world.

1. You are walking along a quiet beach. As you wander the dunes, you spot a surfboard washed up on the sand. Describe the surfboard and the impression it makes on you.

2. You climb onto the board and paddle out to try your luck on the waves. How are the conditions for surfing today?

3. You have managed to get to your feet and are experiencing the thrill of actually riding the wave, when suddenly you wipe out and tumble headfirst into the water. What do you think, feel, or try to scream as you struggle to find your way back to the surface?

4. You finally emerge from the water unscathed, and looking back toward the beach, you see that a person you know has been watching you. Who is that person?

KEY TO "WAVE AFTER WAVE"

(M) ost of us sense intuitively the strong psychological associations between the sea and sex. The way you imagined your experience on the waves tells us something about your expectations and desires in the sexual realm.

1. Throughout history and across cultures, the sea is portrayed as feminine. Against that backdrop, the surfboard provides an overt example of what Freud referred to as a "phallic symbol." Women: Your description of the surfboard corresponds with your image and impression of masculine sexual characteristics. Men: Your answer shows your perception of your own physical sexuality.

"It's just like every other surfboard out there. You've seen one, you've seen 'em all." Either you haven't seen enough surfboards, or you've seen far too many.

"It's a monster wooden longboard, freshly waxed and gleaming, with a red stripe up the middle." Thanks for sharing, but that's just a little more than any of us wanted to know.

"A sad-looking, beaten-up old board that nobody wants anymore." Don't rush to judgment. Who knows? A little wax, a little buffing, and that old board might look as good as new.

2. The surfing conditions you described reveal your own hopes and expectations from sex.

"The water is warm and inviting. Wave after wave breaks softly on the beach." That's enough to put anyone in the mood.

"The water's a little chilly, and there's not a wave in sight." Don't worry, there will be other days, other chances. Maybe today you can just snuggle up in a beach blanket.

"Towering surf! A fifty-foot tsunami! Cowabunga, baby!!!" Down, boy! Heel!

3. Total submersion within the churning waters is a metaphor for the peak of sexual pleasure. Your thoughts and feelings as you struggled upward correspond to those you experience in the throes of ecstasy.

"Oh, damn—I almost made it that time! I was so close!" I take it you were expecting something more from the experience?

"Help! Somebody please help me! I can't breathe!" Hopefully some-body around here knows mouth-to-mouth.

"Hey, this isn't so bad. I think I'll just stay down here and have a swim around until the wave passes." Don't get too comfortable down there. You're going to have to come up for air *sometime*.

4. The person you pictured standing on the beach is someone you show intense interest in, in a sexual sense. This doesn't necessarily indicate active sexual desire; it may be that you're simply curious

about what that person is like in the most intimate and unguarded of moments. Then again maybe, just maybe, that's something you want to find out firsthand.

Was the person you named your current lover or a secret love interest? That shouldn't be too hard to accept. But then there are always those who name a member of the same sex, a cousin, their dentist. . . . Don't worry, your secrets are safe with us.

BUILDING A NEW TOMORROW

The clock struck twelve, the ball dropped in Times Square, and the sound of champagne corks popping was heard around the globe. And after all the buildup, hoopla, and hype, after the apocalyptic anxieties and eager anticipation, the world somehow managed to find its way safely into the new millennium. Looking back, we can see that the prophecies of doom were overblown and the Y2K bug seems like little more than a ploy to sell system upgrades. But we, the last children of the twentieth century, all shared for a moment that sense of newness and opportunity—the chance to make a world better than the one we inherited and create a legacy to share with our children and theirs over the next thousand years.

1. You are working for an urban planning corporation and have been assigned to the community development team for a major new millennium project. You have been asked to come up with an inspirational theme for the city. What theme do you propose?

2. The project team has a number of members, each with a certain set of experiences and skills. Why do you think you were selected to participate in this project? (Give as many reasons as you like.)

3. What kind of person is the project manager? Describe his or her personality and qualities as a leader.

KEY TO "BUILDING A NEW TOMORROW"

(T) owns and cities are natural symbols of social life. Most of the cities we are familiar with sprang up unplanned and spread outward and upward in a seemingly random fashion. But this scenario asks you to deliberately plan a city for the future, giving your mind the chance to express its vision of an ideal setting for human interaction. Your answers reveal your approach and feelings about the social world around you.

1. The theme you selected for the new city is something you feel is absolutely essential to your own happiness as a member of society. And for most people, that means the very thing they sense is most sorely lacking in their environment at present.

Was your theme something ideal, like "harmony," "peace," or "Mother Nature"? We all feel the need for more of those these days. Or did you pick something along the lines of a cartoon fantasy world where everyone smiles all the time and the sun is always shining? That may actually be an easier goal to achieve, but you're facing some strong competition in Orlando, Anaheim, and Tokyo.

2. The reasons you gave for being picked for the team are strengths you see in yourself that no one else recognizes. That may be because those "strengths" are not quite as strong as you might like to think. The people around you are the most objective judges of

your potential. Don't be afraid to listen to what others have to say about your abilities—their evaluations can steer you away from the dead-end streets of overconfidence and self-deception.

3. The team manager reveals your own image of yourself in the future. Do you see yourself developing into a supportive, motivated, and inspirational leader, or a harsh and unreasonable slave driver? If it's the latter, you may want to start reconsidering the particular path to personal development you're currently heading down. Even Scrooge got the chance to repent.

DWELLERS OF THE DEEP

T he undersea world holds mysteries we can barely conceive. Its seemingly endless waters remain the last great frontier on earth, luring adventurers, challenging science, and inspiring poets, artists, and the romantic at heart. The simplest explanation for this allure is that there is more to the ocean than meets the eye. Hidden beneath its featureless surface, millions upon millions of creatures—some familiar, some fantastically strange—live, feed, breed, and die. It is almost as if our planet contained two separate worlds, which have only just begun to discover each other.

Within the box on page 36 is a picture of a coral branch. This exercise requires you to draw an octopus (or more than one) anywhere within the box.

DWELLERS OF THE DEEP

The modern-day world holds mysteries we can barely conceive. In an age of endless adventure—where remain the last great frontier on earth waiting adventures, challenging, scares, and inspiring postal service and the possible. It hasn't. The time for exploration for this distant planet is nearer to the ocean than to the sky, but has remain far fewer than ventured millions upon millions of nation. Some further some genuinely, so atmospheric food, bread and die. It is almost if it can place; certainly a bit separate words, we may have only read begin to scratch each other.

With the last page 36. It is from life, the good deed. This exercise requires you to think and deeper for once more than any where to our life box.

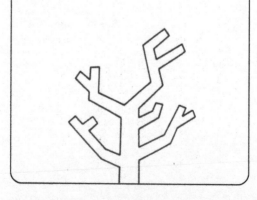

KEY TO "DWELLERS OF THE DEEP"

(C) arl Jung, one of the founders of psychoanalysis, observed that the octopus, with its sinister, alien appearance, slippery invertebrate form, and tentacles that stretch in all directions, is a commonly encountered symbol of stress and anxiety. Your artwork sheds some light on the level and nature of stress in your life.

The size and number of octopuses you drew reflect the importance and number of worries in your life. A single huge octopus indicates a preoccupation with a single great concern, while a number of smaller octopuses swarming everywhere is a sign that you feel overwhelmed by minor stresses and annoyances on all sides. If you drew a small, friendly-looking creature bobbing happily beneath the waves, good for you! No one said that life has to be a cold, dark abyss.

The position of the octopus in relation to the coral is also significant. If you drew a free-floating octopus, it means you believe that your stress, however great it may be, is resolvable. But if you drew the octopus clinging tightly to the coral, it shows you feel as if you're locked in a stranglehold of entanglements.

STAR MATERIAL

A rranging the schedule, approving the wardrobe and makeup, setting up interviews, and handling the fans—the work of a celebrity's personal manager is never done. In this line of business, image is everything. If you want to keep the media buzzing and the lenses of the paparazzi trained, if you want to keep the calls for talk show appearances and concert bookings coming, you need to make sure your client looks the part twenty-four hours a day, every day of the year. The rest of the time, you can relax.

You are the manager of an up-and-coming band. They've got the look, they've got the talent, but for some reason, the records just aren't selling as well as you know they could. Why do you think they haven't been able to make their break into the big time? Give the one reason you see behind their lack of popularity.

KEY TO "STAR MATERIAL"

(P) erhaps a manager's most important function is to size up a client's strengths and weaknesses with a cold, objective eye and order the changes that need to be made. By placing yourself in the role of a manager, you took on this same critical perspective. And that piercing gaze quickly located a shortcoming that you have seen but may have been unable consciously to acknowledge in yourself.

Did you say the problem was bad timing, lack of connections, or simply an industry-wide slump in record sales? It's easy to blame all your failings on the outside world, even in your subconscious. Perhaps what you're really trying to say is that your greatest weakness is your inability to accept responsibility and take charge of your destiny.

If the problem was turmoil or infighting among the members of the band, it's likely that you too are plagued by inner conflicts. If you want to be a star, first you're going to have to become your own biggest fan.

If you felt the problem was that the band didn't pay enough attention to their fans, you might want to try taking better care of the people in your life. Remember, it's the people who love you that made you into the star material you are.

HEIGH-HO!

G rumpy, Sneezy, Dopey . . . Doc . . . Happy . . . Sleepy, and . . . what'sisname. Few of us can name all of the seven dwarfs in "Snow White," but the tale just wouldn't be the same without them. After all, they took Snow White in and gave her a place in their home, drove off the evil queen, and kept her lifeless body in safekeeping until she was revived by true love's kiss. We know that Snow White went on to live happily ever after, but whatever became of those seven little fellows?

It is the final scene of "Snow White," and she is riding off into her new life with her handsome prince. You have the power to read the thoughts of the seven dwarfs as they send her off. What are their true feelings at that moment? (It isn't necessary to make your answers conform to the personalities of the dwarfs as they were depicted in the story; just describe seven individual reactions to the scene.)

KEY TO "HEIGH-HO!"

(D) on't feel Bashful if you couldn't remember the name of that seventh dwarf. Your mind is a very big place, and things are bound to get lost in there from time to time. Most of our minds are so big, in fact, that they play home to a number of entirely different personalities and ways of looking at the world. The ways that you pictured the dwarfs reacting to Snow White's departure illuminate your own true nature and its multiplicity of perspectives.

Did all seven dwarfs wish her well and send her off without hard feelings or regrets? You are decent to the core. If the Magic Mirror judged hearts instead of faces, then *you* would be the fairest one of all.

Or did one or more of the dwarfs mutter something like "That ingrate! After all we did for her! That'll teach me to go out of my way for someone." Too much time in the mines has started to darken your perspective. Maybe you should try whistling while you work.

The amount of diversity in your seven answers also gives an indication of your level of self-integration and internal consistency. If they all ran along the same lines, then, for better or worse, your answers paint an accurate picture of your true character.

If you came up with seven completely different reactions, it could be said that you are capable of entertaining a number of views on any issue. The question you need to ask yourself now is, Which represents the real you?

CAT GOT YOUR TONGUE?

A dog may be man's best friend, but a cat always seems to be its *own* best friend. You may love them or hate them (as if they cared either way), but cats have shared as long a history with us humans as any species of animal on earth, and it's safe to say that they'll be around for ages to come. It's not that cats actually do much for people—they can't fetch the newspaper, shake hands, or play Frisbee—or perhaps it's just that they choose not to. But their cool indifference, quiet pride, and utter impenetrability seem to justify them a place in our world regardless.

We all have our individual perceptions about the cat. Which of the following four phrases strikes closest to the image you hold?

1. Basking in the sun.
2. Mysterious and inscrutable.
3. Pleasantly soft to the touch.
4. A companionless creature.

KEY TO "CAT GOT YOUR TONGUE?"

I n Jungian psychology, the cat is a representative of the feminine principle known as the *anima,* or your true inner self (as opposed to the social role you play). The description you selected as applying best to cats reveals the nature of your own true self, in its positive and negative aspects.

1. Basking in the sun.

In describing a catlike activity, rather than the cat itself, you show a sensitivity toward the natural actions of things within their environments. This makes you an accepting and easily acceptable person, capable of getting along well with everyone you meet. On the positive side, this means that people perceive you as comfortable in almost any situation. But that same uncanny sense of comfort can also make you appear to be a little superficial or unconcerned with others.

2. Mysterious and inscrutable.

You instinctively chose to describe the cat in terms of its personality, almost as if it were human. And the attributes of the cat's character that drew your attention are precisely the ones you share with it. Your true inner self is a kaleidoscope, changing and renewing itself constantly. This makes predicting your behavior an endlessly intriguing challenge to the people who love you, but it can also make you seem like more trouble than you're worth to those without the time or inclination to ponder riddles and enigmas.

3. Pleasantly soft to the touch.

To you, the cat presents itself as a physical object, defined specifically in terms of how it affects you. You see the world as something created to stimulate and serve you. This tendency may manifest itself as an aura of calm self-assurance or simply as excessive self-involvement. But it's likely that until you perceive that it has some direct effect on your life, this insight will be of no interest to you either way.

4. A companionless creature.

You define the cat in social terms, showing the emphasis you place on the role of the individual within (or apart from) the group. And your choice of "companionless" to describe the cat's condition is more than a little tinged with feeling, a sense of loneliness that the animal itself does not necessarily share. You are most deeply attuned to the emotional and social realms, making you appear caring, warm, and genuinely concerned about others. But it can also make you seem somewhat overly sensitive and melodramatic when you give full expression to your feelings.

RIDING THE RAILS

M ost of us approach a ride on the subway with a mixture of fascination and dread. They're crowded, they're noisy, and they aren't famous for their safety or hygiene, but there's something about subways that makes them an integral part of the urban experience. Maybe it's the hum of the electrified rails or the jerky rhythm of sudden starts and stops as the train hurtles from station to station. Or maybe it's their endless ability to surprise even the most hardened city dweller with outrageous shocks and unforeseeable encounters. Whatever it is, subways seem to tempt us with the promise "You thought you'd seen everything? Well, you ain't seen nothing yet."

You're riding on a crowded subway when you see that a single seat has opened up nearby. You are just about to sit down when you notice another person has also begun moving toward the same empty seat. What do you do?

1. Take the seat, of course.
2. Hesitate and look around before doing anything.
3. Let the other person have the seat.
4. Move to another car.

You are riding on a crowded subway when you see—but a single seat has opened up nearby. You are just about to sit down when you notice another person also coming toward the same empty seat. What do you do?

1. Take the seat anyway.
2. Offer the seat to the other person. Be polite and kind.
3. Let the other person have the seat.
4. Lean over the other person.

KEY TO "RIDING THE RAILS"

I t may not be the most glamorous way to go, and you can't expect much of the view, but sometimes a trip on the subway is the only way to get where you're going. In that sense, subways are a lot like blind dates. And in both situations, it isn't always easy to change course once you've started heading down the wrong track. The way you saw yourself confronting the problem of taking the seat corresponds to the way you would act when you wanted to turn down a second date after a friend had gone to the trouble of introducing you to someone they "just know would be perfect for you."

1. Take the seat, of course.

You know what you want and, just as important, what you don't. Experience has taught you that it makes no sense to agonize over the repercussions for others when it's you who has to live with the consequences. This means you may hurt a few feelings as you go through life, but at least they won't be your own.

2. Hesitate and look around before doing anything.

You always look at the big picture and consider the feelings of everyone involved before making a decision. After all, the world doesn't revolve around you. Just remember, the decision you make now may mean the difference between a comfortable seat and a long ride spent wondering how you ended up on the end of a strap.

3. Let the other person have the seat.

You worry too much about what other people think, and in wanting to look good, you end up acceding to the wishes of others. People praise you as being extremely easy to live with, but if you don't stand up for yourself once in a while, you could be in for a very long trip down a very dark tunnel, stuck with someone who's only too happy to let you stand the whole way.

4. Move to another car.

The very concept of the blind date is alien to you. The prospect of being thrust into a relationship with someone you've never met is enough to make you start reaching for the emergency brake. Fortunately, the people who know you have already figured this out, and despite your many fine qualities, you aren't likely to be at the top of any matchmaker's list of prospects.

THE MIRROR DOESN'T LIE

C lothes shopping provides us with the rare opportunity to confront stark reality in the form of a full-length mirror. We've all been there—the outfit that looked great hanging on the display floor rack undergoes some disturbing metamorphosis on the way back to the fitting room and leaves you standing in clothes that were clearly intended for someone other than you. Then, at that very instant of recognition, the curtain draws back and the sales assistant peeks in to marvel, "Wow, that looks *great* on you!"

How do you respond to this clash of realities?

1. Give a straight account of your opinion: "You've got to be kidding. This looks terrible on me."

2. Point out the specific reasons you don't like the outfit: "The collar is too wide and I don't like the way the sleeves bunch up at the cuffs."

3. Disregard the comment: "Thanks, but I think I'll look around a little bit more."

4. Accept the compliment and say: "Do you really think so? All right, I guess I'll take it."

KEY TO "THE MIRROR DOESN'T LIE"

S hopping for new clothes can be likened to a spiritual quest, a time for critical self-assessment as you search for the perfect means to express your true identity. Your wardrobe is an extension of yourself, selected in the hopes of highlighting your best features, physical or otherwise. The way you responded to the clerk's bald-faced flattery reveals the aspect of your self you esteem most dearly.

1. "You've got to be kidding. This looks terrible on me."

Mirrors don't lie, and they have told you that you look good often enough that you can do without empty praise. Your greatest pride is in your appearance, and you aren't about to let some sales clerk in search of a commission spoil the look you've worked so hard to achieve.

2. "The collar is too wide and I don't like the way the sleeves bunch up at the cuffs."

You may not look perfect all the time, but you refuse to be made to look like a fool. You know the power of your mind to perceive the world clearly, and that intellectual pride won't stand being lied to. Your personal style is an expression of refined sensibility and keen powers of discrimination, and you wouldn't dream of compromising that for any reason.

3. "Thanks, but I think I'll look around a little bit more."

Your philosophy is "I'm me, other people are other people," and you never let the two get confused. There is no central source of pride in you, unless it is that you're proud of your unique existence. In the end, you just go your own way and let others think, say, and do as they please.

4. "Do you really think so? All right, I guess I'll take it."

You haven't yet located a source of pride within yourself—if you had, you wouldn't let people manipulate and deceive you like that. It's time you took another honest look in that mirror—you might just be surprised to find that you like what you see. Besides, paying for all those unwanted outfits can get to be a very expensive habit.

READING YOU LIKE A BOOK

Y ou can tell a lot about people from their reading habits. Some are very fussy about their books, refusing to read anything outside of a particular genre or subject matter. Others read indiscriminately, devouring volume after volume without pattern or preference. Many read only on occasion or when work or study demands it. And then there are those who simply don't read at all if they can avoid it.

But for those who do read, not just out of necessity, but for the sheer pleasure and relaxation it affords, finding a good book is almost like making a new friend. There's a sense of simultaneous familiarity and discovery. It's as if a window has opened into a previously unimagined world, but one you sensed was waiting for you all along. Sometimes it's almost as if the book has chosen you.

1. A book lies open in front of you. What type of story does it contain?

2. You begin to read and soon find that you yourself are a character in the story. What kind of role do you play?

3. You read further and come to a section where the pages have been damaged, making them nearly impossible to read. What part of the story is it?

4. You have just closed the cover after finishing the book. How was the ending?

KEY TO "READING YOU LIKE A BOOK"

(W)hile reading habits and preferences may vary widely from person to person, we all share a common experience in which books and reading were an inevitable part of life: our school years. In our culture, books and school are inextricably linked, and the answers you gave in response to this scenario likewise echo your own experiences during school.

1. The type of story you imagined reflects your general impression of your school years.

Does your answer suggest you lived through a comedy, a mystery, or a romance? Then again, who among us didn't?

Or perhaps it was an erotic novel? Either you were a very precocious child or you had an overactive imagination.

A Shakespearean tragedy? The fact that you survived all five acts has added nobility to your character.

2. The role you saw yourself in is the image you have of yourself in your time as a student.

Were you the star of the tale? A sidekick? Comic relief? Or no more than a bit player with only a single line of dialogue on page 283? It may just be that your character was being developed for the sequel.

3. The scene described in the damaged pages mirrors a situation in which you were hurt during your youth. Broken hearts can hurt

as much as an act of violence, and even seemingly minor traumas can take a lifetime to heal. Although at first there might not seem to be any immediate connection to your life, if you think back to your past, it's more than likely you'll find some buried painful memory associated with the scene.

4. The ending of the story is an expression of your feelings of closure (or a lack thereof) regarding your days spent at school.

Did you answer something like "And they rode off into the sunset to live happily ever after"? A little clichéd, perhaps, but you can't argue with success.

Perhaps you envisioned a story in which your character dies in the end? It's likely you greeted your graduation as a chance to be reborn into a new life.

Or was the ending a cliff-hanging "To be continued . . ."? In a way, that's the most accurate response you could give. You'll just have to wait and see how the next episode turns out.

SPILL THE WINE

An elegant French restaurant: the mood is just right, the maître d' arrived with a fine bottle of red wine, and now, after approving the vintage and performing the obligatory swish test, you are ready to raise your glasses and share a toast between lovers.

But as you lift your glass, your arm jerks and you spill wine on the white tablecloth. From the list below, describe the way the wine spilled.

1. The tablecloth is completely soaked in wine.
2. There are several large red splotches.
3. A few drops of wine spilled out here and there.
4. Fortunately, there's only one small spot on the tablecloth.

KEY TO "SPILL THE WINE"

W ine and other alcoholic drinks are associated in the mind with feelings of sexual desire (but not necessarily performance). The way you imagined yourself spilling the wine shows how you perceive your own sexual drive and your ability to keep it under control.

1. The tablecloth is completely soaked in wine.

Your sex drive is operating at 200 percent capacity. We'll let the people who should know best answer as to whether that's a good or a bad thing, but you really should try a little harder to make sure more of that wine of yours reaches its intended target.

2. There are several large red splotches.

Your answer suggests that you feel strong sexual attraction to a number of different people. Attraction is one thing, acting on it is another. Don't let your desire to sample every bottle in the cellar intoxicate you. True connoisseurs have learned to appreciate quality without ever needing to swallow a sip.

3. A few drops of wine spilled out here and there.

You exhibit normal curiosity, but do a good job of reining in your sexual energies, which helps you to avoid trouble and potential embarrassment. If you're quick with your napkin, there's no reason anyone even has to know about those little stains.

4. Fortunately, there's only one small spot on the tablecloth.

Either you have better than average reflexes when it comes to cutting off embarrassing faux pas or there just wasn't much wine in your glass to begin with. Either way, your sex drive is no match for your table manners.

[YOUR NAME HERE]

The world is full of other people, and their number grows day by day. For most of us, our social worlds also expand a little each day. Most of our contacts with others are random, chance encounters with people we may never meet a second time. But sometimes fate has other plans, and the stranger you met just yesterday may change your life tomorrow. That uncertainty is one of the things that keep life interesting. Yes, each of our circles of acquaintances is constantly expanding. But when you take a moment to reflect, you may be surprised at how that circle is not as wide as you might have thought.

(For this exercise, you'll need a blank square sheet of paper and a pencil or pen.)

1. First, write your name in a box in the center of the paper.

2. Next, try to fill the remaining blank space on the page with the names of people you know. Take as long as you need, but try to fill in the entire page.

3. Now, draw a single horizontal line through the center of the page. It should cut through the box with your name in it.

4. Finally, choose a name at random in each of the two sections of the page and circle them both.

KEY TO "[YOUR NAME HERE]"

(R) andomness is a simple and familiar concept, but one the
mind has difficulty achieving in practice. Even a conscious
and honest attempt to make a random selection is never truly free
from the influences of subtle biases and unconscious preferences.
The names you picked from the crowded page were determined at
least in part by your own perceptions of the people named and
how you position them in relation to yourself.

The name you circled in the upper half of the page belongs to
someone you respect or see as standing above you. The person
whose name you circled in the bottom half is someone you take for
granted or look down on. You may be surprised to find that these
feelings are in no way related to whether or not you like the people
in question. Love and respect do not always go hand in hand.

WHERE THE SKY MEETS THE SEA

T here are breathtaking mountain vistas, sweeping metropolitan skylines, rugged tracts of forest that stretch as far as the eye can see, and gentle country landscapes dotted with fields and farms, but of all the scenic views in the world, none can stir the imagination and calm the soul like the unbroken line where the sky meets the sea. That blue horizon is a vast space inviting the mind to relax and unwind, to soar above and dive within, to dream. . . .

You are staying at a resort hotel with an ocean view. Lying on your bed, you gaze out a huge bay window across the cool blue waters, and lulled by the scene, you drift off to sleep. Which of the following views greets you when you awake?

1. A bright midday sun burning over the sea.
2. The dark ocean sleeping beneath a starry night sky.
3. A cool mist rolling in over the waters.
4. The sun just beginning to sink beneath the horizon at dusk.

KEY TO "WHERE THE SKY MEETS THE SEA"

(I) n myths and ancient religions from around the world, the sea and the sky are pictured as an eternal couple, forever holding each other in a loving embrace. The way you envisaged the scene out your hotel room window is your vision of the ideal relationship between two loving partners and shows the things you seek most from love.

1. A bright midday sun burning over the sea.

Passionate excitement and intensity are essential to your ideal romance. For you, love isn't true love if it doesn't burn like a fire, and if that means added danger, it always proves worth the risks in the end.

2. The dark ocean sleeping beneath a starry night sky.

Others may think you're a little hokey or old-fashioned, but you place the greatest emphasis on things like commitment and faithful devotion in a relationship. Your love affairs may not set the sky ablaze, but they will never cause you any sleepless nights, either. And when other loves have clouded over or burst into flames, you will still be enjoying those nights of untroubled sleep—together.

3. A cool mist rolling in over the waters.

The line between friendship and love is blurred for you; the two inevitably flow into each other. Your perfect relationship is with someone you can tell your secrets to, share laughter and tears with, and just relax and be yourself around. You refuse to believe that your lover can't also be your best friend.

4. The sun just beginning to sink beneath the horizon at dusk.

You seek a storybook romance that inspires the world with its picture-postcard perfection. Everything has to be just right, from the meeting, to the first kiss, to the place settings at the wedding, to the house with the white picket fence. True love is a once-in-a-lifetime experience, and you see no reason to settle for less than the very best.

IF THE SHOE FITS

F or many people, finding the right pair of shoes is more than just an excuse to go shopping, it's an obsession. After all, shoes are incredibly important. It's an article of faith to the fashion savvy that footwear puts the finishing touch on every ensemble, and no outfit can survive a poor choice in shoes. And any athlete can tell you that the shoes may not make you run faster, jump higher, or drive the ball farther, but at least you'll look and feel good doing it. And for all of us, there are few better feelings than that first day spent in a pair of comfortable new shoes. Yes, although we may not give them much notice, shoes hold a curious power over our lives.

Imagine that you are a comfortable pair of shoes. If you could pick any person to wear you, who would that person be?

KEY TO "IF THE SHOE FITS"

(W) hen you imagine yourself as another person's shoes, you mentally place yourself in the position where they literally step and walk on you. This image is associated with feelings of self-negation, surrender, and subjection to the will of another.

The person you named as your wearer is someone you can easily imagine yourself utterly enslaved by or would be happy to devote yourself to, body and soul.

Did your response surprise you? Don't be alarmed; there's no shame in wanting to be totally dominated. Well, maybe just a little shame, but that's part of the thrill, isn't it?

SKIMMING THE SURFACE

We humans excel at many things. However, floating isn't one of them. Sure, with a little practice and a lot of effort we might manage to keep our heads above water for a few laps in the swimming pool, but none of us would fare very well if dropped in the middle of the ocean without a life preserver. But, as always seems to be the case, human ingenuity has made up for the short-comings of the body and provided us with boats. And thanks to those seaworthy craft, now there is no spot on the surface of the world's waters that lies beyond our reach.

Imagine that you are a boat floating on the water. Which of the following best describes you?

1. A raft of rough-hewn logs.
2. A sturdy rowboat.
3. A racing yacht.
4. A cruise ship.

KEY TO "SKIMMING THE SURFACE"

(S) hips and boats are most at home when surrounded on all sides by nothing but water, unimpeded by obstructions or boundaries of any kind. Picturing yourself as a boat on the open sea conjured a similar image of life unfettered by restrictions or limits. The type of boat you saw yourself as is linked to the ways you prefer to spend those precious moments when your time is truly your own.

1. A raft of rough-hewn logs.

You spend your free time drifting from place to place and enjoying outdoor activities. Your interests range from intense sports like kayaking and rock climbing to relaxing pastimes like camping, fishing, and simply wandering about. The important common thread is a natural setting, and you might be just as happy to spend a day lying on your back in the grass, staring up at the clouds.

2. A sturdy rowboat.

Nothing relaxes you like working up a healthy sweat, and it shows in the ways you spend your days off. High-impact, low-impact, team sports, or solo, you love the way it feels to put your body through its paces.

3. A racing yacht.

What better way to spend a lazy summer afternoon than racing around at breakneck speed? Up-tempo recreations are your preferred mode of entertainment, whether they take the form of fast-paced sports, high-stakes gambling, or games requiring split-second timing.

4. A cruise ship.

Everyday life is exciting enough as it is, and slow-paced, cerebral activities are just what the doctor ordered when you have time to unwind. A game of chess or a crossword puzzle, a leisurely walk, a nice long book, perhaps a game of shuffleboard—these are the things that you look to when you while away the hours.

MAKE A WISH

Y ou can't have everything. That may seem like a statement of the obvious, but it's surprising how many people seem to forget the fact when making their decisions. Something in human nature refuses to accept that universal rule. We want to believe we can have it all, if only because it makes for a pleasant fantasy. You can dream what you like, but even if you were the wealthiest person on the planet, there would be some things your money couldn't buy. The secret to true contentment lies not in trying to satisfy every craving or desire, but in learning to be satisfied with the things you have. That is a reality of sharing the world with others. But what if it weren't so?

Imagine that you have discovered a magical lamp. A genie appears when you rub it and offers to grant you a single wish in return for setting it free. You can wish for anything in the world you want (with the standard wish granter's stipulation of no wishing for more wishes). What do you wish for?

KEY TO "MAKE A WISH"

$\left(\mathrm{T}\right)$ he things we wish for are things we think we want most from life, but more specifically, they are things we think we cannot obtain by ourselves. The thing you wished for is something you hope to receive from someone else and corresponds to what you want most from your partner.

Did you ask for fabulous riches or treasure? That wish may someday come true, but many find in acquiring wealth by attaching themselves to another that they are forced to give up something much more valuable than they could ever hope to gain.

Or was your wish for something more intangible, such as limitless power, stunning beauty, or sheer physical pleasure? Reflect on the ways you go about seeking a lover. You may find out too late that pleasure fades, beauty withers, and power corrupts.

Those who wished for wisdom or contentment are already well on the way to finding those wishes come true. The key is only to stop looking for those things to be given you and to discover them within.

DANCING WATERS

Fountains add a touch of magic to any public space. The fine mist carried onto the breeze, the gentle sounds of water falling into water, the sparkle of light as it plays on the rippling surface: it's enough to transform a humdrum little park into a fantasy setting. Perhaps that's why the local fountain is such a popular meeting place for romantic assignations and getting together with friends.

Close your eyes and imagine a park with a fountain. You have arranged to meet some friends there before a night out on the town. What kind of fountain do you see?

1. A single jet of water blasting straight up in the air like a geyser.
2. A number of medium-size fountains in a sparkling array, their spray dissolving into droplets of mist.
3. A smallish, burbling fountain.
4. An intricately engineered and complex water sculpture.

KEY TO "DANCING WATERS"

(T) hey may be impressive, enchanting, even magical. They may inspire romance or sheer awe. But one thing you can't say about fountains is that they're practical. The water goes up, the water comes down—what does it achieve? Nonetheless, we sense that the world would be a poorer place without them. Sometimes you need to forget about practicality and just cut loose and enjoy. And therein lies the key to this scenario: The type of fountain you imagined is related to the way you spend your money when enjoying a night out with friends.

1. A single jet of water blasting straight up in the air like a geyser.

You're like a magician with money, able to make vast quantities disappear in the blink of an eye. It doesn't matter much to you the way that you consume it, just as long as you don't leave any leftovers. This makes you everybody's friend the first weekend after payday and explains why people around the office have taken to calling you "Old Faithful."

2. A number of medium-size fountains in a sparkling array, their spray dissolving into droplets of mist.

You like to use money to impress, spending it in a flashy way to guarantee maximum effect. You have been known to order food you don't even like, simply because it was the most expensive thing on the menu. As long as you're willing to keep paying the tab, there will always be people willing to act impressed.

3. A smallish, burbling fountain.

You are a conservative spender—that is, on those rare occasions when you spend anything at all. You figure the sales tax for everyone's bill when you split the tab and *then* whip out your coupons. Your spending habits definitely aren't going to make you go broke, but if you don't loosen up those purse strings a little, you may find yourself going solo.

4. An intricately engineered and complex water sculpture.

You're a schemer, always trying to make more out of your money than was there to begin with. You count convincing a waitress that you qualified for the kiddie meal discount when you were fifteen as one of your proudest accomplishments. It's not the money itself that's at issue, it's just a medium you use to express your creative impulses. That may earn you a bright future in trading stock options, but getting thrown out of a movie theater for sneaking in the emergency exit is not a good way to score points on a date.

HAPPY LANDINGS

Every day, people pay good money for the privilege of stepping out the door of a moving airplane and plunging to earth. Skydiving isn't for everyone, but the statistics tell us it's actually a low-risk venture, considerably safer than, say, trying to cross against the light in Manhattan traffic. But even knowing that, we have a hard time finding a rational explanation for the act. Some say it's the adrenaline, but for veteran enthusiasts, that purely physical rush has worn off after the first few jumps. The thing that really keeps calling them back is those brief few minutes of perfect clarity as the natural world lies spread out in miniature beneath their feet, with everything put into proper perspective. Yes, the old-timers will tell you, it's not the thrill of the jump, it's the view on the way down.

You are in mid-descent, floating slowly earthward under the canopy of your open parachute. Describe the view as you look down.

1. A field of grass and flowers.
2. A craggy, rocky landscape.
3. Wild animals waiting with open jaws.
4. A flowing river.

KEY TO "HAPPY LANDINGS"

T hey say that the fall doesn't kill you, just the landing. And the image of the landing that awaits you shows your general attitude and expectations about what the world holds in store for you. The scene you selected reveals your level of optimism or pessimism toward life.

1. A field of grass and flowers.

You are the eternal optimist. You can probably smell the flowers from eight thousand feet and were pleased to note that the grass was growing especially thick to cushion your fall. At this altitude, life is beautiful; just don't get so engrossed in the view that you forget to tuck and roll.

2. A craggy, rocky landscape.

You think Murphy was an optimist: when nothing can go wrong, it will anyway. Well, at least your chute hasn't gotten tangled. Yet. You should try looking more on the bright side of things. After all, right now you're on top of the world. The only place to go is . . . down.

3. Wild animals waiting with open jaws.

You don't mind that the world is out to get you, but only because it's so fun to watch. You view your fate with a kind of resigned bemusement and never pass up the chance for a laugh, even when it's at your own expense.

4. A flowing river.

You are neither pessimist nor optimist, but take things as they come and deal with problems as they arise. You recognize that no one knows enough about the future to decide whether it will be "good" or "bad," and besides, you've got enough things to concern yourself with right here in the present. Specifically, like whether or not to aim for the riverbank to reduce the risk of drowning or angle toward the deepest part to soften the crunch of impact.

WHO'S TO BLAME?

Take a moment to reflect on your romantic history. How many times have you said, "This is it. I've finally found my one true love"? And how many times has the reality turned out differently? Paperback romances and fairy tales promote an ideal of a first and only love, but few of us can claim to have had such uncomplicated good fortune. For most people, the process of finding the perfect partner is one of trial and error: breakups, makeups, missed opportunities, and misunderstandings. Human love is a fragile creation, and sometimes the smallest thing—the wrong choice of words or a single clumsy gesture—can make love shatter, stall, or fade away.

Think of the last three people you have loved in your life, and write down the reasons each of those relationships ended (or failed to begin). Try to be as specific as possible in giving the reasons. For example, in a case of unrequited love, state whether it didn't work out because the other person didn't notice your signals or just wasn't interested, or whether it was because you lacked the courage to say how you felt. In completing this exercise, avoid vague, noncommittal statements like "It just wasn't meant to be," "It wasn't really anybody's fault," or "We were both a little bit at fault." Take as long as you need to answer, but assign the blame to one side or the other in each case.

KEY TO "WHO'S TO BLAME?"

(B) eing the judge in the court of love is not always easy. Were you able to render a final verdict in each case before you? Some people can dash off a list of reasons as fast as they can write. Others take much longer to deliberate before arriving at a decision.

The key to this exercise is not an analysis of the content of your responses, but the time you spent deciding on them. The amount of time it took you to assign and accept blame reveals your attitude toward and aptitude for romantic love.

By definition, breakups and rejections are negative experiences. People who are able to produce reasons without much hesitation are focused too intently on the negative aspects of their love lives. They may be rich in experience but have yet to derive any real benefit from it. If you fall in this category, you need to concentrate more on the positive side of things before you can hope to attain or inspire happiness in love.

The inability to assign blame quickly actually reveals a tendency to remember the good and forget the bad, which is an important ingredient in the recipe for success in love relationships. You may have hurt others, or been hurt yourself, but on the whole you see your romantic past as a series of positive learning experiences. For you love is, as it should be, an enjoyable opportunity for growth.

A Perfect Ten

Looks: 10
Brains: 10
Personality: 10

Few people get the chance to meet someone who matches that description, but it's nice to believe that somewhere out there, there's a perfect ten. Someone who makes the sun shine a little brighter just by getting out of bed in the morning. Someone it would be an honor just to be in the same room with. But how would you approach such a charmed individual? What could you possibly talk about? The prospect of encountering true perfection is a little intimidating, but in the end, wouldn't it be enough just to stand back and admire the view?

Picture in your mind the ideal woman: strong and gentle, graceful and wise, beautiful in every sense. Which of the situations below best fits your image of her?

1. She is exploring the streets of some exotic locale.
2. She is engaged in a romance with an equally ideal lover.
3. She is standing on a stage, basking in the spotlight as the crowd calls out for more.
4. She is behind the wheel of a high-performance sports car.

KEY TO "A PERFECT TEN"

I t may be because we all carry some idealized image of our mothers from infancy, or it may be that women are just naturally closer to perfection than members of certain other genders. Whatever the case, it is a fact that people tend to find it easier to imagine a perfect woman than a perfect man. In envisioning this ideal person, you opened your mind to your own potential for perfection. The setting you selected was the one that you felt was best suited to a perfectly fulfilled individual and corresponds to what you see as the nearest route to achieving your own self-realization.

1. She is exploring the streets of some exotic locale.
     You associate human perfection with situations where mood and the ability to stir the emotions play a primary role. You place similar emphasis on the feeling side of your nature, and the road to self-realization is leading you to a career as an artist or creator. Let your dreams be your road map, and they'll never lead you astray.

2. She is engaged in a romance with an equally ideal lover.
     Your preferred sphere of activity is the world of human relationships. All of our paths through life intersect with the paths of many others, and your success in particular will be determined by your strength at forming partnerships, forging alliances, and building networks of personal connections.

3. She is standing on a stage, basking in the spotlight as the crowd calls out for more.

You are at your best in situations that allow you to exercise your personal magnetism and charismatic charm over a group. You have the power to fascinate and inspire, and even if you choose not to play the part of a star, someday you may find that role is thrust upon you.

4. She is behind the wheel of a high-performance sports car.

You demand control over your destiny and can't be satisfied with sitting still. These qualities are what make you so impeccably suited to the role of leader. You may have to take the first step by declaring your independence and striking off on your own, but rest assured, one day you will be the one making the decisions and giving the orders.

SNIP

H and most people a pen and paper and ask them to draw something specific, and they will draw it for you without a second thought. But give them the same pen and paper and ask them to draw anything they like, and most will freeze up for a moment. Sometimes the prospect of total freedom makes us hesitate more than the most challenging obstacle.

You have a single sheet of paper and a pair of scissors. You've been asked to cut the paper into two halves in any way you like. How do you cut the paper?

1. A clean cut straight down the middle.
2. A line curving back and forth several times.
3. A jagged-edged cut.
4. A single gently rounded curve.

KEY TO "SNIP"

C utting off a relationship is much like cutting a page in two. There's no reason either of the processes needs to be complicated—a few quick snips and you're done. But things don't always work out so easily in real life. It could be simple clumsiness born of haste, but often there's more to it than that. Sometimes making a clean cut just doesn't seem to suit the situation. Sometimes we like to get creative, to express the way we really feel.

1. A clean cut straight down the middle.

When you end a relationship, you really end it, without hand wringing, regrets, or remorse. This stems from your belief that clean cuts are the most painless and heal without leaving scars, a surgical principle you apply with cold, objective precision in all realms of your life. As a result of that "right down the middle" approach, you have probably managed to accumulate a few half sets of cutlery, some mateless chairs, and an encyclopedia that only goes up to M.

2. A line curving back and forth several times.

You agonize over your decisions, fretting endlessly over how to ensure that no one is left feeling angry or hurt. But playing the waiting game only prolongs the agony for you and everyone involved. Sometimes you vacillate so much that it makes your head spin. Breakups are hard enough as it is, there's no reason they have to make you seasick, too.

3. A jagged-edged cut.

Maybe "Rip that damn paper into tiny pieces" is a better way to describe how you exit a relationship. You don't burn your bridges—you blow them up. To your way of thinking, the phrase *happy ending* is an oxymoron. And in the spirit of fairness, you try to make sure that everybody gets their share of the grief.

4. A single gently rounded curve.

The hopeless romantic in you prefers "au revoir" to "adieu," and you never see the logic in breaking up when it's obvious that all you both need is to spend some time apart. But don't forget that not everyone shares your undying sense of optimism. Sometimes "It's over—I never want to see you again" means just that.

WHEN THE PARTY'S OVER

Y ou drew the short straw and ended up with the unenviable task of being designated driver for the night. You resign yourself to a long night of club soda and cocktail nuts and manage to make it all the way to the agreed-upon twelve o'clock final round. But your jolly companions have different ideas, and with eyes out of focus and beer on their breath, the call goes out for "Just one more for the road!"

Nobody likes to be a wet blanket, but you've had enough. What do you say to convince your drunken friends that it really is time to go home?

1. "If you stay out any later, there's going to be hell to pay when you get home."

2. "If I don't get home soon, I'm going to have to sleep in the dog-house."

3. "You've had enough already. Let's go before you make yourself sick."

4. "Come on, party's over. I've got to get up early tomorrow."

KEY TO "WHEN THE PARTY'S OVER"

(T) here's a reason they call it "baby-sitting a drunk." Drunks are like children in many ways: they laugh and cry at the silliest things; they have difficulty finishing their sentences; sometimes they even wet their pants. But the most relevant similarity in this scenario is that both can be a nightmare to control for the people who are supposed to be responsible for them. The way you tried persuading your partying friends to call it a night tells us something about your current (or future) parenting style.

1. "If you stay out any later, there's going to be hell to pay when you get home."

You don't want your children to think of you as an ogre, but sometimes the coercive power of a believable threat is too much to resist. That's the nice thing about having a partner. You can scare the kids into behaving with, "Just wait till Dad gets home!" or, "Mom is going to freak when she sees this mess," and still come away looking like the nice half of the good cop/bad cop routine. But you can't always be your kids' best friend. Sometimes you have to settle for being their parent.

2. "If I don't get home soon, I'm going to have to sleep in the doghouse."

You take the "best pals" strategy (see #1, above) to the next step, asking your kids to protect you from the consequences of their misbehavior. But in this approach, not only do you turn your spouse into the bad guy, but by abdicating all responsibility, you relinquish your own authority as well. It may be time for a refresher course in Parenting 101.

3. "You've had enough already. Let's go before you make yourself sick."

Your no-nonsense, "stick to the facts" approach may not win you any nominations in the "Coolest Parent Ever" awards, but you always have your kids' best interests at heart. And in the long run, that more than anything else will earn you their love and respect.

4. "Come on, party's over. I've got to get up early tomorrow."

You have a tendency to put your own priorities ahead of those of your kids. Parenting involves self-sacrifice, and that isn't always easy to do. But once you've drawn that straw, it's a reality you're going to have to come to terms with. Who knows, you may even learn to love it.

A LITTLE HORSE SENSE

atching a trained horse and rider, you can easily get the impression that the two have somehow been fused into one. Learning to ride a horse is not an easy thing to do, but for those who have mastered the equestrian art, the experience is its own reward. There's a thrill in having a powerful steed respond instantly to your every command, and the finest riders admit that when they're in the saddle it's almost as if the horse has become an extension of their own bodies.

If you were a rider in a horse show and could select your mount, what kind of horse would you choose to be seen on?

1. A graceful steed with muscles rippling beneath its shining coat.
2. A Thoroughbred of unquestionable lineage.
3. A lovable companion with a sensitive, knowing gleam in its eye.
4. A one-in-a-million horse that's not only intelligent, but beautiful as well.

KEY TO "A LITTLE HORSE SENSE"

(A) horse is a horse, of course, of course—unless, of course, it's a subconscious representation of your own sexual self-image. In choosing the horse you wanted to be seen on, you based your selection on the things you most want potential lovers to notice in you. The type of horse you picked corresponds to what you see as your own strongest sales point in attracting members of the opposite sex. Of course, how the rest of the world sees things is sometimes another matter entirely.

1. A graceful steed with muscles rippling beneath its shining coat.

You are most confident in your own appearance: beautiful skin, great body, perfect hair. You know you look good, and you feel good about it. That confidence may even be borne out by the facts, but whether it is or not, you should realize that the best riders choose their mounts for qualities other than just the way they look on the show grounds. Come race time, you're still going to be expected to perform.

2. A Thoroughbred of unquestionable lineage.

Sophistication and good breeding are what distinguish you from the crowd. Or so you believe. But what you see as marks of an elite background may actually make you seem just a little spoiled or full of yourself. True breeding is reflected in character. And that's something you'll have to let the rest of the world find in you for itself.

3. A lovable companion with a sensitive, knowing gleam in its eye.

You want to be known for your sense of humor, sparkling conversation, and lively wit. There's no doubt that you're good at engaging in banter and making small talk. But remember—sometimes jokes build bridges, and sometimes they build walls. It might be wise to take a look around you from time to time and see if you're the only one who's laughing.

4. A one-in-a-million horse that's not only intelligent, but beautiful as well.

Whatever your weak points may be, lack of confidence isn't one of them. You may in fact be beautiful and smart. You might even be charming, funny, and athletic to boot. But that high assessment of yourself can also serve to put distance between you and the rest of us mere mortals. Don't try so hard to impress people. You don't need to prove anything. After all, if not for that overconfidence, you might just be perfect.

SWEETS FOR THE SWEET

W e've all heard the story of the little girl and boy lost in the woods who stumble upon a house made of tempting sweets. And even when we know that it's a trap laid by a cunning witch, it's hard not to sympathize with those hungry children as they begin to pick away at the cookie doorknobs, candy glass windowpanes, and sugar-frosted roof shingles. After all, what child (or adult, for that matter) could be expected to resist such a treat?

Imagine you are lost in a dark forest and starting to feel the first pangs of hunger when you come across a cottage made of sweets. After checking the area to make sure no witches are lurking about, you get ready to dig in. How do you set about consuming the house?

1. I'd just start eating everything in sight.
2. I'd try sampling as many different kinds of sweets as I could find.
3. I'd find my one favorite sweet and stick to that.
4. I'm not very into sweets. Actually, I'd prefer some crunchy mixed nuts.

KEY TO "SWEETS FOR THE SWEET"

(C) andy and snacks are not something you give much thought to in preparing, or eat only at set mealtimes. Most of the time, it seems they just end up in your stomach without your knowing how they got there. Personal relationships have a similar way of forming without conscious planning or deliberation. But that's not to say that subconscious preferences don't play a role. On a behavioral level, the way you approached the candy cottage mirrors your approach to the world of friendships.

1. I'd just start eating everything in sight.

You are always up front and out in the open in dealing with the world, almost like a child in your innocent enthusiasm. This straightforward approach makes you easy for others to understand and accept, but you should realize that not everyone is as forthright and honest as you. Sometimes that honesty of yours makes you just a little too trusting, and you have been known to rush in where angels wouldn't dare to tread.

2. I'd try sampling as many different kinds of sweets as I could find.

The world is full of people, and you wouldn't mind the chance to meet them all. You are a true master at finding the good qualities in others. But your desire to have a little taste of everything can also be read as an unwillingness to get too deeply involved with any one person. While it's good to be able to enjoy all kinds of tastes, there comes a time when you're going to have to finally admit to someone, "You're the sweetest of them all."

3. I'd find my one favorite sweet and stick to that.

If you can find even a single person in the world who shares your interests, tastes, and aspirations, that's enough for you. It is indeed a wonderful thing to be able to find a person who sees the world exactly as you do, but by limiting yourself to a single flavor of relationship, you may be cutting yourself off from a whole world of delicious experiences.

4. I'm not very into sweets. Actually, I'd prefer some crunchy mixed nuts.

For you, the word *crazy* has a positive connotation. Accordingly, your circle of friends and acquaintances has more than the average number of interesting characters. The life of an outsider has its appeal, and you enjoy the perspective that taking a step back from the crowd affords you. But in trying to set yourself apart, you may sometimes be seen as someone who's trying too hard to be different. It's important to remember that the people who are most afraid of being thought ordinary are those to whom that description best applies.

ALL HEAVEN'S CHILDREN

There are some things that are difficult to accept outright, but which we want to believe in nonetheless. Kindly fairies, mysterious ghosts, Santa Claus. The concept of heavenly angels in particular seems to capture the imagination, and few people are willing to deny the possibility that they exist. It's comforting to think of them looking down upon us with goodwill and compassion, ready to aid us in our darkest hour of need. And what harm could possibly come from having a little faith in divine providence?

Imagine that you are an angel, pictured in the box on page 95. As you soar through the heavens, you hear a fallen angel (or several) calling out to you. How many angels do you see, and what are they saying to you? Draw a picture of the angel(s) and write their words in the empty space in the box.

A small object, perhaps a fallen angel, is a world of elegance—or both. All of this goes that cight after a stage in which it is the most weighty, at leaving in number of the work generation. This element is sexualized in human sexuality. The also forms the basis for resolving the [...] hips, and other pleasant relations. It is crucial to be absorbed in some way together with one of you in your own. [...]

The size and number of the Other angel are [...] a happy in our lives is attraction to members of the same sex. The greater the size and number, the stronger your desire [...] long as often are. The greater of the angel to others reflects how at ease you are showing the warmth of the attraction you desire. A small [...] angel surrounding you [...] one other amount to individuals may feel at a closer struggling with [...]

"In order of the angel's wings, your angels are an expression. The ... from the number/tone [...] the warmth you hold your own [...] or waver on [...] their call number [...] the meaning of freedom or understanding. This could be your [...]

KEY TO "ALL HEAVEN'S CHILDREN"

I n depth psychology, the fallen angel is a symbol of same-sex love. All people pass through a stage in which they are most actively interested in members of the same gender. This interest is not limited to homosexuality, but also forms the basis for strong loving friendships and other platonic relations. It is normal to be attracted in some way or another to people of your own gender. Your responses to this exercise show just how deep and strong those attractions are in you.

The size and number of the fallen angels you drew is a gauge of your level of attraction to members of the same sex. The greater the size and number, the stronger your interest, latent or otherwise. The positions of the angels in relation to the picture of your angel also show the strength of the attraction. If you drew a crowd of angels surrounding you, or one close enough to touch, you may feel as if you are struggling with temptation on all sides, or that the object of your desire is tantalizingly within your reach.

The words of the angels calling out to you are an expression of the voice of your own subconscious. If they taunted you with cries of "Why don't you come and join us? You're missing out on the real fun down here!" or "Don't be so high and mighty. This could be you someday," it indicates a certain curiosity (or at least a willingness to hear more) about alternates to the orthodox paradise. But if the angels only rejected you—"We don't need your kind around here. Fly back up to heaven where you belong!"—then it's likely you feel little in the way of subconscious desire toward members of your own sex.

If this quiz reveals some unexpected leanings in you or your partner (or both!), we'll let you work that out between yourselves. Just remember, heaven smiles on all forms of love.

TIME FOR A CHANGE

Y ou don't need an interior decorator or feng shui adviser to tell you that sometimes the smallest changes to a room's decor can have a surprisingly large impact. You don't have to replace or rearrange the furniture; merely applying a different color of cushions on the sofa, adding a new floor plant or a print on the wall, or even switching from bright white to soft yellow lightbulbs can utterly transform the way a familiar room feels. Sometimes all it really takes is a good session with the vacuum and a feather duster. Whatever the changes, big or small, they're sure to make you see your home in a new light.

You have decided to buy a new tablecloth for your dining room table. What kind of tablecloth do you want?

1. A simple white tablecloth.
2. A tablecloth in a "warm" color, such as fuchsia, mustard, or apricot.
3. A tablecloth in a "cool" color, like periwinkle, teal, or moss.
4. A tablecloth with a bright, multicolored pattern.

KEY TO "TIME FOR A CHANGE"

We're all decorators within, letting our hearts decide the way we want our surroundings to look. The dining room is a center of home life, and the table represents the stage across which many family dramas play out. Perhaps without realizing it, you chose the tablecloth you did for more than just the way it fit the color scheme. Your choice also reveals the atmosphere you want to create, or the thing you place most importance on, in your family life.

1. A simple white tablecloth.

Whether it's a father who's always shouting to keep the volume down, an ongoing marital dispute over bathroom rights, or just the feeling of being hemmed in by the endless responsibilities of raising a family in a busy world, the things you sense your home lacks most are personal space and freedom. That white tablecloth might help a little, but for real elbow room there's nothing quite like a move to a bigger house.

2. A tablecloth in a "warm" color, such as fuchsia, mustard, or apricot.

Your home suffers most from a lack of open lines of communication. You may have noticed that family meals are declining in frequency, and even when you do manage to get everyone together, it can be hard to get a discussion going. The condition is serious, but not irreversible. As you intuitively sensed, if you make your home a warm and comfortable place to be together, those family conversations will start to flow naturally again.

3. A tablecloth in a "cool" color, like periwinkle, teal, or moss.

You have a close family, sometimes a little too close for comfort. People can't seem to get out of each other's way in your home, and it always seems as if somebody's toes are getting stepped on. It's admirable that your family is so tightly knit; now, if you could only find a way to turn down the tension level a notch. . . . If that tablecloth doesn't work, a little Mantovani in the background during dinner might just do the trick.

4. A tablecloth with a bright, multicolored pattern.

The environment in your home is sedate. Sometimes you think "comatose" might be a better description. It feels as if your home has become no more than a place to collapse after another long day, and perhaps a little colorful enhancement would provide a much needed shot of vitality. It takes only one person to strike the match that gets the home fire burning again. Maybe that someone could be you.

A DAY TO REMEMBER

The flowers you wore to the prom are faded and brittle, an uncomfortable number of the faces in the yearbook look unfamiliar, and most of the things you learned in trigonometry seemed to vanish from your memory the instant you handed in the final to be graded. But some memories from high school stay fresh in everyone's minds, always readily available whenever the urge for a trip down memory lane should strike.

Think back to your high school graduation ceremony. Which of the following images stands out most clearly in your mind?

1. The face of the principal handing out diplomas and shaking hands.
2. The banner reading "Congratulations to the Class of XXXX."
3. The ranks of students standing proudly in their caps and gowns.
4. The playing of the graduation march.

KEY TO "A DAY TO REMEMBER"

(G) raduation ceremonies follow certain fixed patterns, but ask ten different people to describe their impressions, and it's probable that they'll describe ten very different scenes. People naturally tend to focus on different aspects of the world and therefore find certain types of information easier to recall than others. The thing you remember most clearly about your graduation shows the area where your powers of recall are strongest.

1. The face of the principal handing out diplomas and shaking hands.

You have a special aptitude for remembering faces and names. Meet someone once, and you never need to be introduced again. And that is a skill that has stood you in good stead on more than one occasion, making people you barely know feel like valued friends.

2. The banner reading "Congratulations to the Class of XXXX."

You've got a strong head for figures—birthdays, telephone numbers, batting averages, the number of steps from your front door to the car. You might not remember the name of someone you ate lunch with last week, but you could probably recollect how much you paid for the meal. Those powers of recall have earned you a reputation as serious and dependable. After all, you never forget a date.

3. The ranks of students standing proudly in their caps and gowns.

You don't remember things so much as you reminisce about them. Your ability to recall a scene is inextricably tied to the emotions it aroused in you, and you can almost experience the feelings again just by turning your mind's eye that way. This allows you to replay and enjoy happy memories over and over again. But it also means you have difficulty forgiving and forgetting after you've been hurt.

4. The playing of the graduation march.

Visual memories seem to fade quickly for you, but the things you hear and say are stored in a permanent file that you can access as easily as pulling a CD from the shelf. When your memory of an event is blurred, sometimes all it takes is hearing a snatch of a melody that was playing in the background at the time to cause the memories to come flooding back to you.

WINNING ISN'T EVERYTHING

T eam sports generate as much passion in the stands as they do on the field, and the excitement surrounding a football championship, World Cup soccer match, or final-round basketball playoff is intense enough to send waves of energy around the world. In fact, it's often the case that the fans get more carried away by the action than do the players themselves.

1. You are in the stands at a championship sporting event and the team you are cheering for is defending against a critical drive toward the goal as the final seconds of the game tick away. What do you shout to the players on your team?

2. Your favorite player commits a flagrant violation and is ejected from the game, but only after protesting violently. Describe the referee's demeanor as he sends your unruly hero to the sidelines.

3. Three . . . two . . . one . . . the timer counts down to zero and your team has suffered a disastrous loss. Describe your honest response to this setback.

KEY TO "WINNING ISN'T EVERYTHING"

(T) eam sports are a form of cultural ritual in which the human needs for aggression and conflict are channeled toward a more positive end. Positive as long as your team wins, that is. The way you reacted to your team's performance reveals how you respond to interpersonal confrontations, particularly those you get the worst of.

1. The way you cheered (or jeered) your squad is an indication of how you react when engaged in a heated debate or difference of opinion. Did you offer unconditional support, cheering, "Go team, *go*"? Right or wrong, you're not the type to go down without a fight.

Or did you engage in some criticism from the safety of the bleachers—"What are those bums thinking? My grandmother could play better!" That lack of a loyal fan base may itself be the biggest hole in your defense.

2. The ref's reaction to the foul parallels your own expression when you are in a confrontation with another person. Did he maintain an unruffled, professional demeanor, or did he get carried away in the heat of the moment? As much as we'd like to see refs keep their cool, the men in stripes are only human.

3. Your response to your team's defeat shows how you might respond when you come out on the losing end of an argument.

"You can't win 'em all. We'll get 'em next time!" You may not be cut out for competitive sports—or the debate team—but there's definitely a place for you on the pep squad.

"I've had it with those losers. I'm never cheering for them again." But if you don't cheer for them, who will?

REAL FEAR

The experience of virtual reality has been around for much longer than most people think—we call it a trip to the movies. A good film draws you into another world, playing out larger than life on a panoramic canvas and leaving only a pair of eyes there in the darkened theater to follow the action on-screen. And of all the emotions a movie can evoke, none can grip an audience so completely as fear. There is no such thing as virtual fear. Your heart pounds, your breath comes fast and shallow, your nerves are like live wires, and your stomach rises into your throat. If that isn't real, nothing is.

Everyone enjoys a good scare once in a while. Which of the following thrillers scares the pants off you?

1. A vengeance-crazed woman hunting down and destroying the people she hates.
2. A big-budget disaster flick with passengers trapped belowdecks aboard a sinking ocean liner.
3. A sinister serial killer selecting his victims at random.
4. An unstoppable alien life form wreaking havoc on earth.

KEY TO "REAL FEAR"

$\widehat{W}$ e watch thrillers, chillers, slashers, and shockers because we want to be scared in a safe way. But it isn't necessary to go to a theater or video store to experience fear; the real world is frightening enough as it is. When selecting a scary movie, we don't just want to be scared; we choose to be scared by exactly those things that scare us most. The type of film you selected reveals a source of anxiety that doesn't disappear from your mind after the ending credits roll.

1. A vengeance-crazed woman hunting down and destroying the people she hates.

Inhabiting a world filled with billions of other people scares you silly. The realm of personal relationships is a snakepit of unpredictable reactions and irrational acts. Perhaps you've already been involved in a few horror stories starring friends, family, or lovers, but sometimes you just wish the world would leave you alone and go scare somebody else.

2. A big-budget disaster flick with passengers trapped belowdecks aboard a sinking ocean liner.

You're sensitive to the plight of the passengers plunged from the heights of luxury to the depths of despair because you fear nothing more than an assault on the positive image you have of your life. You want to believe that things can be perfect, and you go out of your way to avoid any suggestion to the contrary. But just as no ship is unsinkable, there's no such thing as a perfect life. But don't let that bother you too much; on that score we're all in the same boat.

3. A sinister serial killer selecting his victims at random.

You seek safety in numbers against an incomprehensible, sometimes hostile world. You fear being separated from the group, where you might make easy prey, and this means you're sometimes too willing to sacrifice your identity in order to fit in. But the only way to make true friends—the kind who will stand by you when danger looms—is to have the courage to be yourself.

4. An unstoppable alien life form wreaking havoc on earth.

You fear that you're being overrated by the people around you, people you see as depending on you to be strong. You don't want to let those people down, but you're afraid that someday there will be a crisis too big for you to handle. Relax, you don't have to be perfect. Accept yourself and your limitations. No one else expects you to be invincible—why should you?

MUSIC BOX

Music boxes are designed for the sole purpose of making people feel good. They call us back to simpler times, lull us to sleep with their delicate tunes, even make us feel young again. All it takes is a few turns of the key. But behind that simple purpose lies a complex mechanism of interlocking cogs, gears, and wheels. Every chime a hammer strikes is also a signal that the tune is winding down toward its end.

You fell in love with a particular music box at an antiques store, bought it on impulse, and took it home. Its melody is beautiful, but one day it suddenly stops playing.

1. How long after you bought the music box did it cease to play?
2. What do you think as you hold the broken music box in your hands?

KEY TO "MUSIC BOX"

(T) he music box is a symbol of beauty and pleasure that is fated to come to an end. But it also represents the repetition of the same old tune over and over again. The way you perceived your antique music box shows some of your expectations from the pleasures of romance and the sense of how it may one day end.

1. The amount of time you thought the music box continued to play corresponds to your expectations of how long love will endure.

Years? A few months? Two or three days? That's such a shame. After all, it takes only a little tender loving care and the music should play forever.

2. The way you felt about the broken music box shows how you feel when a relationship has died.

Did you shrug it off as inevitable and toss it in the trash? Mutter something about the poor quality of the workmanship and curse yourself for wasting your money? Maybe you resolved to go out shopping for a new one right away?

Or did you try to think of a way to get it working again? Sometimes all it takes is one good whack in the right spot.

Some Room for Improvement

G ood real estate brokers understand that whether it's a one-room studio apartment or a three-bedroom Cape Cod with a yard, their clients are looking for more than four walls and a door. They're looking for a place to call home. Model showrooms are designed with that in mind. The interior design and furniture are carefully selected to create a feeling in potential home buyers: "This is where I want to be. This is where I belong."

You have recently been to see a model home and are now mulling over whether or not to sign the lease. The tour was unhurried, and you had the chance to ask the questions you had prepared, but there's one part of the home that you still want to spend a little more time looking over before you can feel comfortable in making your final decision.

Which area do you want to examine again?

1. The bathroom.
2. The bedroom.
3. The dining room/kitchen.
4. The veranda/garden.

KEY TO "SOME ROOM FOR IMPROVEMENT"

I n psychoanalysis, houses are commonly encountered representations of the body, and the search for a new home corresponds to the quest for physical self-improvement. Accordingly, the area of the home that you expressed the most interest in is related to the ways that you seek to improve your own body. More specifically, the space in the home that you were not completely satisfied with shows what factors tend to stand in the way of your diet, exercise, or self-renewal plans.

1. The bathroom.

The bathroom is the place where the body is cleansed and represents the urge toward renewal and purging of the self. You who chose the bathroom as the source of dissatisfaction intuitively sense that your own commitment to a better self may not be strong enough.

2. The bedroom.

Bedrooms are cognitively associated with the desire for physical relaxation and comfort. You who wanted to see more of the bedroom actually wanted to see more of the bed; to kick off your shoes and snuggle under the covers. Your problem isn't with the idea of diets or physical exercise, just with all the work that's involved.

3. The dining room/kitchen.

These rooms have strong associations with the desire for food, and food itself. And those are the very things that leap to the forefront of your mind when contemplating a self-improvement routine. Keeping your figure would be a cinch for you, if you could only eat.

4. The veranda/garden.

The veranda and garden are linked with the relaxation and refreshment of the soul—places to take a break and unwind. If you wanted to see more of the garden, it's likely that you feel you're under constant pressure and stress—stress that can lead to missed workouts, poor eating habits, exhaustion, and lack of motivation. The first step you take toward improving your body may have to be relieving what's on your mind.

Just the Right Fit

An alien entity or maleficent elf sneaks into your closet and drawers at night and, while you slumber, shrinks each article of your clothing by the slightest imperceptible amount. Only after weeks of these nightly visitations do you begin to notice the insidious effects. Pants that once fit comfortably now seem to pinch and confine, zippers and buttons refuse to close, and you have reached the final hole in your favorite belt. Yes, you must be the victim of some sinister clothes-shrinking demon. The only alternative is . . . unthinkable.

All jesting aside, much of the modern world has fallen out of shape. You can try to count calories or cut down on between-meals snacks, but study after study has shown there's only one proven and effective way to win the battle of the bulge: exercise. But exercise doesn't have to be a chore. Fitness centers and gyms have evolved ways to minimize the drudgery while maximizing results, and those who exercise regularly will tell you that a good workout can make you feel great. Believe it or not, there are even those who claim that exercise can be fun.

1. Some time ago, you became a member of a fitness club. But for some reason you stopped going. What was the reason you quit the club?

2. After an extended sojourn in the land of the couch potato, you decide to give routine exercise another try, this time at a different gym. Describe how you set about looking for a new place to work out.

3. While shopping around for a fitness center, you sign up for a free one-day trial session. Describe the appearance of the trial workout instructor.

4. You find a club that's to your liking and embark on a regimen of regular exercise. One day you notice that the gym always seems to be playing the same type of music in the background. What kind of music is it?

KEY TO "JUST THE RIGHT FIT"

I t has been said that sex is one of the best workouts you can give your body. Scientific evidence for that assertion remains scant, but when you get right down to it, who really cares? There are psychological links between physical exercise and physical love as well. Your responses to questions about the search for a good workout were determined in part by the way you go about selecting a sex partner.

1. The reason you gave for giving up on your gym is related to the reason you would lose interest in a lover.

"There was no variety, always just hammering away at the same thing over and over again." An understandable complaint, but there are, after all, certain anatomical limits to what the human body is capable of.

"Too fast paced and intense. I just couldn't keep up." You really do need to get into shape. But don't rush things—that leads only to pulled muscles, back strain, and burnout. There are beginner's courses designed especially for people like you.

"I was just too busy." You may be too busy at the moment, but that might also mean it's time to rethink your scheduling priorities. If you can't find thirty minutes for a quick workout a few days a week, you're probably working too hard.

"I'd exhausted all the possibilities at the facility. There were no challenges left for me there." Gulp. Maybe you should get a job as an instructor.

2. Your search for a new fitness club mirrors the way you go about finding a new partner.

"I'd gather information about as many different places as I could, review the pros and cons of each, and then make an informed decision." Effective? Probably. Romantic? No.

"I'd look for a place that was cheap and easy to get to." That's one way of deciding. But it might not be a good idea to tell them that if they ask how you found them.

"I'd ask a friend to recommend a good one." But what are you going to do if you bump into each other just as you're heading in for a workout?

3. Your description of the exercise trainer putting you through your one-day trial workout reflects the type of person you secretly would like to have a one-night stand with. It's probably safe to say you got someone who looks good in a leotard or spandex bike shorts. But what about those of you who described someone of the same sex? Don't feel too concerned; it's only for one workout. If you don't like it, you're under no obligation to sign up for a lifetime membership.

4. The background music you imagined is the kind of music you would prefer to listen to while having sex. If you aren't listening to it already, you might want to give it a try. Sometimes the right song can give you that little boost you need when you're trying to max out to a new personal best.

A SHOULDER TO CRY ON

For a young child, the first trip to summer camp can be exciting, but it can also be a very frightening experience. The first day, everyone else seems to know what they're doing, to belong to a circle of friends, and to have decided already which bunk they're going to sleep in. But with the help of the counselors and a few newfound friends, most kids seem to make it through that adjustment period without suffering any permanent damage, and it isn't unusual for a child who screamed, "I wanna go home!" on day one to cry, "I never wanna leave!" when the summer finally ends.

Imagine you're a counselor at a summer camp. A young first-timer knocks on your cabin door one night after lights-out and, with tears in his eyes, tells you he wants to go home. What do you say to the child?

KEY TO "A SHOULDER TO CRY ON"

I t's always easier to face sadness, fear, or loneliness when there's someone there to comfort you and say the things you need to hear. But not everyone responds to a cry for help in the same way. It takes a sensitive person to know just the right words to say to another who is feeling down. It almost requires getting inside that other person's mind and feeling their feelings with them. The words you spoke to the frightened child are actually the things you most want to hear when you yourself are troubled.

All some people need is simple reassurance: "Don't worry. Things will look better in the morning. I'll keep an eye out on you and everything will be fine."

Others just want to be told it's all right to cry: "That's right, just let it all out."

Others hate to be pitied: "Look at you crying like a baby. You think no one else is lonely? Grow up and get back to bed."

Whatever your response, finding the person who will say those things that help you overcome your darkest hours will be key to your happiness in life.

AT THE WATER'S EDGE

T he winding river is both a source and a symbol of life. Rivers provide fresh water, transportation, and places to bathe, swim, fish, and relax outdoors, and as a result people have chosen to build their homes near rivers from time immemorial. Of course, there is always the danger of flooding, and the shallows serve as breeding grounds for parasites and hiding places for predators. But humans seem to have found that the benefits associated with natural waterways outweigh the risks, and few riversides today remain unsettled by our kind.

Imagine living in a home located near a river or stream. Which of the following best describes the property?

1. A home on a small island in the middle of a river.
2. A wide stream flowing past the home with a narrow footbridge across it.
3. A babbling brook running through one corner of the property.
4. A home whose property is crisscrossed by a maze of winding streams.

KEY TO "AT THE WATER'S EDGE"

(W) hile rivers may provide access to long-distance transportation by boat, on a personal scale they also frequently serve as impassable physical barriers. The relationship you saw between your home and the water nearby reflects your desire for social distance and personal space.

1. A home on a small island in the middle of a river.

You don't ask for infinite room to roam, just a quiet place to call your own—a place where you can be alone with your thoughts and escape from the pressures of society. If the home is a castle, you'd prefer yours to come with a moat.

2. A wide stream flowing past the home with a narrow footbridge across it.

You keep an intimate circle of personal relations, while holding the rest of the world at arm's length. That may make you a little harder to get close to than others, but it also means that when you call someone your friend, you always mean it.

3. A babbling brook running through one corner of the property.

You don't make a clear distinction between your social and private lives. You maintain an open door policy to the world and think of strangers as friends you just haven't met yet. That openness and spirit of hospitality ensures that come what may in life, you will never have to face it alone.

4. A home whose property is crisscrossed by a maze of winding streams.

You live in the midst of a labyrinthine social network, and you're preoccupied with the complex relationships between yourself and the people in your life. At times you may feel the outside world is always on the verge of flooding its banks, but that same maze of meandering channels also protects you from having any of those myriad streams rush straight in through your front door.

SIMULACRUMMY

I t may seem difficult to believe, but the cloning of mice, sheep, and monkeys is already old news, and the science of genetic engineering continues to forge ahead into never-before-explored territories where the lines between life and chemistry, progress and ethics, become blurred. What was once conceivable only as a plot for a low-budget science-fiction movie has recently become the everyday business of some high-budget biotech companies. And despite lingering doubts and protests, the day when humans are cloned seems to be approaching fast.

You are a scientist working on an experimental process to clone human beings. You have finally succeeded in cloning yourself, and using growth-acceleration technologies (patent pending), you are now the proud creator of an exact replica of your body, right down to the fingerprints. But although your clone is physically indistinguishable from you, it has a flaw in its personality that you do not find in your own. What is your clone's shortcoming or fault?

KEY TO "SIMULACRUMMY"

B y assuming the role of a research scientist, you afforded yourself the chance to inspect your character with the clear, cold eye of scientific objectivity. There are hidden flaws and unexpressed inclinations in our personalities that we studiously avoid noticing or thinking much about, but which refuse to remain entirely out of sight. The idea of a clone provides a screen upon which you can project your own submerged faults and repressed desires in safety. And in seeing them from a third-person perspective, you may begin to realize that they are not buried as deeply as you might have believed.

THE BOOK OF LIFE

T here's a book out there you've been searching for, but even you yourself don't know what it is. No subject, title, or author. No Dewey decimal or ISBN. Just a sense of certainty that when you find it, things will fall into place, and one of your life's great purposes will be fulfilled. Maybe you'll find it in a library or see it listed in an e-mail ad from an online store. You might stumble across a worn copy in the bargain bin in a used-book seller's basement. Or maybe you'll never find it at all. But one thing is certain: That book is out there somewhere. You just know it.

You are idly browsing the stacks of a large bookstore—not looking for any book in particular, just looking. You wander down one aisle and begin to search intently through a tall case of books. What is your impression of the books? When answering, describe your general impression of the books' content rather than naming specific authors, genres, or subject matter.

KEY TO "THE BOOK OF LIFE"

(R) eading can be a pleasurable activity, but no matter how much we may enjoy it, it still requires a certain amount of work. You may be able to leave a stereo or television playing in the background and get on with other things, but reading is an all-or-nothing affair. The working world requires a similar commitment of your time and effort, and the terms you used to describe the books that attracted you as you shopped mirror the things that you seek from your job.

Did you find yourself engrossed in a heartwarming love story or chuckling over a few well-turned jokes? That sounds like a great career; now, if only you can get someone to pay you to do it. Or did you perceive the books as a stimulating intellectual challenge? You're an employer's dream come true, but you run a very real risk of waking up one day and discovering that the only thing in your life is your job.

If the description you gave fits your current work environment, then it is likely that you feel satisfied in your present job. But if the description is the exact opposite of what your job is like, then maybe you need to spend less time browsing through bookstores and more time browsing the "Careers" section of the Sunday newspaper.

TRAUMA CENTRAL

T he emergency ward of a busy hospital is a chaos of wailing babies, patients moaning or struggling to describe their symptoms, and a disorderly procession of doctors, nurses, and paramedics all trying to do their job and stay out of each other's way. It is not an ideal environment for anyone involved, but in life-or-death situations people do whatever it takes to ensure survival. Perhaps the best that can be said for emergency rooms is that they are never boring, and TV producers have learned to bank on the voyeuristic thrill afforded by watching how average people respond in a health crisis.

Imagine yourself in the waiting room of the emergency center at a large hospital. As you wait, you begin to look at the faces of the people around you and recognize several acquaintances of yours among the patients. Match a person in your life with each of the following trauma cases:

1. Head swathed in gauze.
2. Face heavily bandaged.
3. Leg in a cast.

KEY TO "TRAUMA CENTRAL"

(T) he symptoms you associated with various people in your life show what you perceive as weaknesses in those people's characters.

1. Head swathed in gauze.

The head is a symbol of leadership and the ability to take command of a situation. The person you named as having a head injury is someone you feel you cannot trust or follow.

2. Face heavily bandaged.

The face represents the personality itself, and a person you imagined as facially disfigured is someone whose personality you have difficulty accepting or someone you just can't get along with.

3. Leg in a cast.

Legs represent stability and forward movement. The person you saw with a leg in a cast is someone you see as slowing you down or holding you back, either through sluggishness or simple clumsiness.

Did you feel some of these diagnoses of yours were a bit severe? Or maybe it's just uncomfortable to have the truth out in the open. But as all doctors know, the only way patients have a chance of getting better is by recognizing that they are sick.

THE WHEEL OF FORTUNE

C asinos make it their business to have something for everyone. If you can't stand blackjack, you might just love the slot machines. If the slots do nothing for you, you can take in a floor show. If the show is no good, you can always enjoy a cocktail on the house and just soak in the colorful atmosphere. The room is alive with flashing lights, jangling bells, and the palpable smell of money, and sometimes it seems difficult to form a rational thought with all the distractions the senses are offered.

Finally you succumb to the lure of the roulette wheel and the prospect of doubling your fortune in a single spin. You bet everything you have on red. The wheel spins. The ball skitters down. You close your eyes and hold your breath, thinking, Red. Red. Red. Come up red. The croupier cries, "Thirty-one, black!" and you turn and walk away without looking back.

What is your reaction on losing everything to this unkind twist of fate?

KEY TO "THE WHEEL OF FORTUNE"

L as Vegas is famous for two things: gambling and marriage. Both hold forth the promise of a lifetime of happiness to those who are fortunate in their decisions. But there's another side to that glinting coin, a side we don't like to think about much, and it promises only bitter disappointment and shattered dreams. The way that you felt about losing all your money is the way you would feel about a marriage that ended in divorce.

"How could I be so stupid? I'm never going to do that again!" How many times have we heard that before? Should we say "Good-bye" or "See you next time"?

"I guess this just wasn't my lucky day." Don't let it get you down. Even the best hit a slump from time to time.

"Well, I must've used up all my bad luck in one shot. Next time I'm sure to hit the jackpot." That's the spirit. Keep it up, and they're going to name a street after you in Atlantic City.

WHEN YOUR TASTES HAVE GROWN UP

C offee may be the quintessential adult drink. That rich aroma, that slightly bitter edge, that feeling of warmth and mellow anticipation as you blow the steam away before taking your first sip. It's an experience you learn to enjoy as you leave childhood behind and serves as a sign that you have entered the grown-up world. Somehow, despite the caffeine, in the proper setting coffee soothes the nerves and relaxes the mind. A seat in a secluded corner of a coffee shop with a good book and some jazz playing softly in the background provides an ideal environment for many to take a step back from the stresses and strains of work, study, or life itself and enjoy the true luxury of doing nothing at all, if only for the time it takes to finish a cup.

You work hard enough. Take a moment now for yourself and enjoy one of the privileges of adulthood. Will it be French roast? Rich Colombian? A decadent mochaccino? Go ahead—indulge yourself. You've earned it.

1. It's that rarest of occasions, a day with nothing on the schedule, and you decide to enjoy some quality time with yourself in a coffee shop. Describe the atmosphere and ambience of the shop you choose.

2. You order a cup of coffee. What do you do while you're waiting for it to be brought to your table?

3. When the waiter delivers the coffee you ordered, how does it taste, and how is its temperature?

KEY TO "WHEN YOUR TASTES HAVE GROWN UP"

C offee in general and coffee shops in particular are closely linked with ideas of the adult world and social relations. Your responses to the questions in this scenario tell us something about the ways you perceive and manage stress in your own adult relationships.

1. The atmosphere you described is actually what you seek most in your workplace (or school). Some thrive in a lively environment elbow to elbow with other like-minded people. Others value quiet and solitude. Then there are those who don't care what the atmosphere is like, as long as the coffee comes in a bottomless cup.

2. The thing you did while waiting is related to a major source of stress or concern in your life.

Did you just sit and watch the other customers? You're a little too nervous about what others are doing, saying, and thinking. Just be yourself. Everyone else is.

Did you pull out a magazine and start reading, or look at the menu? You may need to get your nose out of the books and try a little more physical activity.

Did you sit and wait without doing anything at all? It's a sign you crave more stimulation from life and are looking for something to occupy your time.

3. How did the coffee taste? The flavor and temperature you imagined corresponds with the level of stress that you needlessly create for yourself. The better your experience of the coffee, the less stress you add to your life. If you imagined it was lukewarm, weak, too bitter, or scalding hot, you make problems where there are none to begin with. In your dreams, you can have anything you imagine—why not at least treat yourself to a nice cup of coffee?

I t can be hard to tell others how you really feel about them. Searching for just the right word or gesture to express your true feelings is never easy, and maybe it's never more difficult than when the person you're trying to address is someone you secretly love. For some, speaking those three little words "I love you" takes more courage than facing the gravest physical threat.

You have decided to admit your true feelings to a person you've loved from a distance for what seems like ages. You have brought a small gift to help show your sincerity and the depth of your love, but when you finally take that leap and offer yourself, that person says, "I'm sorry, but I can't take this from you. I'm in love with someone else."

Oof. Only time will heal your broken heart. The more immediate question is, What do you do with that unwanted gift?

1. Use it yourself.
2. Give it to someone else.
3. Throw it away.
4. Send it by mail to the person who turned it down.

KEY TO "RETURNS POLICY"

(F) ew experiences evoke as strong a reaction as the rejection of love. In extreme cases it can transform a simple passionate longing into a passionate longing for revenge. What you did with the rejected symbol of your love shows the degree to which you are able to recover and get on with your life or tend to linger in a world of broken dreams. This coincides with the levels of acceptance and persistence that you show in dealing with life's setbacks.

1. Use it yourself.

A stoic, you face reality head-on, and like a stoic, you prefer to keep a reminder of your heartache until it fades with the passage of time. You can be honest with yourself in saying, "That hurt," because you know you have the strength to take the pain and wear it like a badge of honor. But what you see as a demonstration of character can also be read as a way of taking revenge by never letting the other person forget how much he or she hurt you.

2. Give it to someone else.

You try to make the most of a bad situation by ridding yourself of an unpleasant reminder and simultaneously making another person happy. You don't put all your eggs in a single basket, and that gives you the freedom to forget about setbacks quickly and get on with life. And even though things may not have worked out to your liking this time, there is bound to be someone out there who will fall in love with the fundamental goodness of your nature.

3. Throw it away.

You may think that by throwing away the gift, you're throwing away all the memories and pain associated with it as well. But you are actually the type who dwells most deeply on hurts and rejections, unable to let go of the past. You may toss that ring in the river only to have it come out of your faucet the next morning. You can't throw away memories or pain, only learn to live with them.

4. Send it by mail to the person who turned it down.

You seek closure for yourself, even if it means ignoring the wishes of a person you thought you loved. This approach may actually be the healthiest for you because it lets you say, "I did everything that I set out to do. The rest was beyond my control."

LOOK OUT BELOW!

Keeping plants offers us the chance to give without any promise of reciprocation, gratitude, or reward. It's true that they ask for little—just some water and sunlight—but in a material sense they give even less in return. Nonetheless, houseplants enjoy a popularity that seems out of proportion to any decorative function they might perform. Perhaps we keep them because they fill a very human need: the need to be needed.

A potted plant you've been keeping on your balcony falls over the ledge it was sitting on. You run outside to survey the damage. What do you see?

1. The plant landed on the ground upright and intact.
2. The pot broke, but the plant seems to have survived the fall.
3. The pot and plant are both smashed beyond recovery.
4. For some strange reason, there is no sign of either plant or pot.

KEY TO "LOOK OUT BELOW!"

(T) he sheltered life of a potted plant corresponds to a hidden, guarded side of your character and the ways you try to keep the world from penetrating your social mask.

1. The plant landed on the ground upright and intact.

You appear to be strong and confident and are always eager to demonstrate your coolness under fire. But beneath that tough facade is a person more concerned with keeping up an image than actually living it.

2. The pot broke, but the plant seems to have survived the fall.

You seem calm and unflappable to others, but the reality is you just hate to show your emotions. Those pent-up feelings within you just keep growing and growing, and no pot can hold them in forever.

3. The pot and plant are both smashed beyond recovery.

You seem to be soft-spoken and self-effacing, but that "natural listener" is crying out for a chance to shine center stage. You are only waiting for an opportunity to break out of the self-imposed mold that confines you.

4. For some strange reason, there is no sign of either plant or pot.

You excel at generating excitement and making others laugh, and people see you as the life of the party (even when there's no party in town). But that glib exterior hides a seriousness and even a shy side that you choose not to show the rest of the world.

FORE!

G olf is not something you can try on the spur of the moment; getting started in the sport is a major decision. It takes practice, patience, and preparation. You need the clubs, the shoes, the funny clothes, and of course the people to play with. Sometimes just getting to the point where you can finally tee off seems like more trouble than it's worth. But many first-timers find, as they settle into their stance with the sun on their backs and get set to address the ball, that all that work and waiting seem justified.

You are a novice trying your first full round of golf. You've hooked, sliced, hacked, whacked, and mulliganed your way through so far. It hasn't been pretty, but with some determination and after a little timely encouragement from your partner, you finally manage to sink the ball in the eighteenth hole. How do you feel now that you've completed the course?

KEY TO "FORE!"

S ports, which combine physical exertion and physical pleasure, are psychologically associated with sex. The way you felt on completing your first day of golf echoes the way you felt after your first sexual encounter.

"Hey, that was actually pretty fun. I guess it really isn't just for old men." Now you're starting to get the picture. You probably thought those old-timers were doing it just for the exercise, didn't you?

"That's it? I don't see what all the fuss is about. I've got better things to do with my time." Like many of life's pleasures, golf is an acquired taste. You might learn to enjoy it after a few more tries.

"I'm hooked. I'm definitely going to do this again next Sunday." Why limit yourself? Some people even find the time to do it more than once a week.

OODLES OF DOODLES

S choolchildren understand that page margins were made for doodling. It's almost sinful to let all that empty white space in a notebook go to waste. Scribbles, squiggles, googly-eyed faces, and hearts with arrows quickly grow and multiply, crowding into the writing space midpage. Give a child a notebook, a pencil, and sufficient time (say, the length of a history lesson on the Triangular Trade), and that boundless imagination spills forth onto page after page. We're taught that doodling is a bad habit, and the notebooks we keep as adults are neater (if duller) for it. But wouldn't it be a little sad to see a student whose notebooks were filled with page after page after page of neatly printed notes and flanked by clean margins on both sides?

Imagine you are a child, doodling happily away. You have begun to draw a picture of a bear. Which of the following looks most like your art?

1. A bear snoozing away contentedly.
2. A bear with its arms raised in a frightening pose.
3. A mother bear leading her cub.
4. A cute bear, like a stuffed toy.

KEY TO "OODLES OF DOODLES"

(I) n the psychology of animal imagery, the bear is a symbolic instance of the archetypal Great Mother. The characteristics of the Great Mother are as diverse as the different types of mothers. The aspect that you emphasized reflects your personal experience of motherly care. This experience plays a somewhat different role in the minds of women and men. For women, the bear you saw yourself drawing is your image of yourself as a mother or the kind of mother you expect to become; for men, it is the image you have of your own mother. Whether you are a man or a woman, this image may play an important part in your selection of a mate. They say that men end up marrying women who remind them of their moms, and women are drawn to men who bring out their maternal instincts.

1. Sleepy bear.

Your image of the mother is relaxed and easygoing, free to be herself and giving that same freedom to her children. She may not keep the neatest of dens, but her home is a place where you always feel welcome and safe to snuggle in for a long winter's nap.

2. Scary bear.

You see the mother as a powerful force, possibly even to the extent that she dominates the home. All mothers want what's best for their children; some demand it. Like it or not, in her family, this mother knows best.

3. Momma bear.

You have an idealized image of the mother: caring, loving, and tender. It may be stereotypical, but it's a nice stereotype to have. But try to have more reasonable expectations for real-world moms. After all, bears don't have to rush home from work in time to pick up the cubs from soccer practice and get dinner in the oven.

4. Cuddly bear.

Your image of the mother is someone who can't necessarily be relied upon, except to be lovable. As much as she may want to play Mommy, it seems that more often than not it's her own children who end up taking care of her. But as hopelessly adorable as she is, no one seems to mind.

TEN GRAND

T en thousand dollars just isn't what it used to be. Twenty years ago, it could have bought you a new car. Fifty years ago, it could have bought you a house. Nowadays, it might get you a nice ten days in Hawaii for two or a remodeled kitchen. Still, the prospect of an extra ten grand is nothing to sneeze at.

Imagine you have won $10,000 in a random sweepstakes drawing. What do you do with the money?

1. Save it until you think of something you really want.
2. Surf that wave of good luck right down to the racetrack and put the whole $10,000 down on a horse.
3. Blow it all on an extravagant party to celebrate your good fortune.
4. Take that romantic trip abroad you've always dreamed of.

KEY TO "TEN GRAND"

Winning a sweepstakes is like suddenly falling for someone—you can't make these kinds of things happen, they just happen to you out of the blue. But true love is something earned. Unlike infatuation or simple physical lust, it demands hard work and dedication. The way you reacted to your sudden good fortune shows your worst habits in love.

1. Save it until you think of something you really want.

You seem to be cautious and serious, but it's because you're always looking out for number one. You don't let yourself get caught up in too much feeling for others, and your partners may end up feeling that you are always on the lookout for something better. The best investment you can make in a relationship is investing yourself.

2. Surf that wave of good luck right down to the racetrack and put the whole $10,000 down on a horse.

They say you can't have too much of a good thing, and you take that argument to its logical conclusion. "If one lover is good, then two must be better, and three, four, ten, even better than that! The sky's the limit!" I don't want to jinx you, but that lucky streak of yours is bound to end sooner or later.

3. Blow it all on an extravagant party to celebrate your good fortune.

Money is made to be spent and love is made to be, well, made. You don't waste precious energy weighing the costs and benefits or comparison-shopping. But you need to consider saving a little something for the future. A real love can last forever, but no party can.

4. Take that romantic trip abroad you've always dreamed of.

You seek your pleasures in foreign places but also want the security of being able to return home when you're done. You feel that your diverse experience has broadened you as an individual and helps to sate your insatiable curiosity. But your habit of spending too much time in exotic ports of call might just get you quarantined by the domestic authorities when you finally make it home. You want it both ways, but love requires you to put down permanent roots.

FROZEN IN TIME

I n fantasy, we can be all-powerful—invincible in conflict and irresistible in love—an omnipotent force in an imagined universe where even the laws of physics cease to apply. Imagine flying, moving mountains, traveling to the far side of the galaxy at faster than light speed. The mind can do these things without breaking a sweat. Our bodies are confined by limitations and laws on all sides, but in our imaginations, we can be free.

Imagine you have a single chance to freeze time and walk about the world as if it were a wax museum. You can do whatever you like. Just what is it you would like to do before the clock's hand thaws?

KEY TO "FROZEN IN TIME"

J ust as the body is bound by the laws of physics, behavior is itself ruled by social constraints. Freud called the part of the mind that monitors the self's unacceptable urges "the superego." The superego is most concerned with real behavior and operates much more weakly in the realm of fantasy. The things you saw yourself doing in a world where laws no longer apply to you show how powerful your own superego, or moral conscience, is. It's been said, "Character is what you do when you think no one else is looking." But the one gaze you can't avoid is your own.

If you merely took the chance to travel for free, snoop around some exciting forbidden location, or just play a good practical joke, it shows a consistency in your standards that speaks of normal moral character. But people who took the opportunity to commit more serious crimes such as stealing a large sum of money or doing harm to others have revealed that their behavior is ruled more by social laws than a strong internal standard.

If you decided that you would keep the world in permanent suspension, so that you could wander it freely forever, you might want to give that decision a little more thought. A frozen world is inevitably cold.

WHO'S GOT THE BUTTON?

H ow do you make your choices when shopping for clothes? Are you lured by certain colors or patterns? Do some brands have the power to make you reach for your credit card? Or are you an inveterate bargain hunter who can't resist the chance to save 40 percent, even if it's something you don't really want or need? Think of the clothes that are already in your closet. You may see patterns other than paisley, tartan, and flower print begin to emerge. Specifically, think of your favorite blouse or shirt. Now visualize the number of buttons on the front. How many buttons are there, and how do you keep them buttoned when you have the shirt on? (Choose the nearest answer from the choice below.)

1. It has more than five buttons down the front, and I button them all.

2. There are two or three buttons on the front, and I button them all.

3. There is a row of buttons on the shirt, and I leave one or two at the top unbuttoned.

4. There are no buttons on the shirt.

KEY TO "WHO'S GOT THE BUTTON?"

(F) ew people consciously make button count a deciding factor when choosing their wardrobes. But as in most matters of taste, the subconscious plays an important role. There are many things in life that are uncontrollable, but there are also some in which we have the power of final say. Buttoning is one. Deciding how we spend our money is another. Both behaviors are ways of expressing one's sense of freedom or control, and your buttoning habits actually reflect the way you handle your finances.

1. It has more than five buttons down the front, and I button them all.

You are very conscientious with your money, never splurging or spending recklessly. Regardless of your income, you set a budget, follow it, and somehow manage to put something away as well. Some might call you tight, but you're on the straight-and-narrow path to financial security.

2. There are two or three buttons on the front, and I button them all.

You take a middle-of-the-road approach in managing your personal finances. You aren't afraid to spend on the things you want, but you don't like to throw money away frivolously, either. You are one of those rare people in control of, and not controlled by, their money.

3. There is a row of buttons on the shirt, and I leave one or two at the top unbuttoned.

You have specific goals and invest every spare penny in them. On the other hand, you're a moderate spender in areas not directly related to realizing your dreams. That single-minded sense of purpose makes you a prime candidate for conversion one day to the buttoned-down look adopted by people who are used to getting what they want from the world.

4. There are no buttons on the shirt.

Your fiscal motto is "A penny saved is a penny wasted." You charge like a wounded bull, and don't look back to survey the damage. Get used to the jeans and T-shirt look. If you keep up the pace, that might be all you're able to afford.

KEEPING THE PEACE

P arks and playgrounds are intended to be places for quiet relaxation and childhood games, but they can be the stage for some less pleasant scenes as well. Kids will be kids, and sometimes that means bad little kids. The child's world is not all hopscotch and hide-and-seek—there are plenty of other ways to pass the time when teachers and parents aren't around.

Walking past a small playground one day, you see two young children engaged in a serious-looking fight. No other adults are around. How do you respond (if at all)?

KEY TO "KEEPING THE PEACE"

(A) fight between children is difficult to ignore—you know it's not really your business, but still, the urge to intervene is strong. Something about the situation seems to invite the voice of reason to speak out and set things right. The same could be said of illicit love affairs between adults. The way you responded to the fighting kids shows the way you might respond if you learned that a friend was having an adulterous affair.

Did you step in and try to break it up? ("Look at the two of you. You should know better!") Or did you just shrug it off and ignore it? ("Let them go at it. It's just part of the growing process.")

There's no one correct answer to the dilemma of whether to break it up or let it slide. But ask yourself, If it was my child, would I want someone to step in? Chances are good that most other people feel the same.

A FLASH OF RED

F rom red as a rose to red as a beet, when we see red it affects us emotionally. Scientific experiments have shown that people asked to remain in a room with red walls become more passionate, aggressive, and easily aroused than people in rooms with muted backgrounds. Research has even shown that exposure to red can make the body temperature rise. Red may be at the low end of the spectrum of light, but it has power to move us like no other color.

Imagine three women, each of whom is fond of the color red and uses it to accent her appearance. The first of these women has her nails painted red, the second wears red lipstick, and the third has her hair colored the same shade. Now imagine their personalities and describe each in detail.

Key to "A Flash of Red"

(A)lthough in some ways we all react similarly to the color red, there are also significant differences in our psychological responses. This is not simply a matter of taste or acculturation but seems to have roots that sink deeper into the mind. In the natural world, red is the universal sign of danger, a way for one animal to let potential foes and competitors know, "Careful, I bite and I'm poisonous." But this same shade is also powerfully seductive, and for animals attuned to the same sexual frequency, it can signal that the mating season has begun. In nature as in fashion, it's not the color itself; it's what you do with it.

The images you had of the three red-accented women reveal the kinds of women you view as friend and foe. This results in different interpretations, depending on whether the respondent is male or female.

Female respondents.

The woman with red nails is seen as a threat and represents the type of woman you can't imagine yourself ever getting along with. On the other hand, you feel a strange and compelling attraction to the woman with red lips. The woman with red hair is an image of the type of woman that you hope you will never become.

Male respondents.

The red-nailed woman is the kind of person you fear will use or make a fool of you, while the red-lipped woman is the type you can imagine yourself falling wildly in love with. The redheaded woman represents the type you can't see yourself being attracted to, no matter how physically beautiful she may be.

FUNNY BUSINESS

I t's easy to laugh at other people, but making others laugh is a different story. There are some people who will do anything to achieve that end, but few of us are willing to resort to making fools of ourselves for a chuckle. True comics have mastered the balancing act of tickling the funny bone without either inflicting pain or injuring their own dignity. A good sense of humor is a rare commodity and consistently rates as the attribute most people look for in their partners and friends. Shared laughter brings people together and leaves a bond rooted in the knowledge that someone else out there got the joke.

1. You are making your debut as a stand-up comedian. You want to be a hit, but there is one person you definitely don't want to show up to watch you perform. Who is that person?

2. What do you see as the single most important ingredient in determining success in the comedy business?

3. During your act, you made a single blunder. What kind of mistake was it, and how did you attempt to recover?

4. One member of the audience laughed harder and longer than anyone else. Who was this fan of yours?

KEY TO "FUNNY BUSINESS"

L aughter is rich in psychological associations of anxiety and escape, control and subversion, while the idea of a stage implies an audience, which also implies being watched and evaluated by others. Against this background, assuming the role of the comedian allows you to place yourself in the position of exposing your fears and weaknesses for the world to see.

1. Who was it that you didn't want to see your act? A lover? One of your parents? Your boss? You might think that you chose them because they were the butt of a number of your jokes, but actually that person is someone you wish never to disappoint or show weakness to. There are some people in life we just don't want to have laughing at us.

2. What did you name as the secret to success as a comic? The thing you saw as essential is something you feel you need more of to succeed in your own social relations. Perfect timing? High-energy performance? A good manager? Those things are important, but perhaps it all boils down to always knowing what people want to hear.

3. The mistake or flub you made mirrors a major blunder from your own past that you have always regretted. If you said you dropped the mike midact, you have probably had more than your share of clumsy accidents. Those who had no response for a heckler have

had bad experiences getting flustered under fire or when being criticized. If you said you offended the audience, it's likely you tend to blurt out the first thing that pops into your head without thinking about who may be standing within earshot.

Your attempted recovery represents the way you think will help you to avoid or minimize the effects of similar mistakes in the future. You can try to ignore it and get on with your routine, but sometimes the best recovery is just to admit your goof and laugh at yourself.

4. Joking is a psychologically complex phenomenon. In one sense, it involves having the power to control others through the ability to make them laugh. But that power can be exercised only by acknowledging and catering to the other's sense of what is funny and involves assuming a risk of failure in the attempt to please. The person you named as your biggest fan is someone you do not want to have power over you. This may be out of a sense of friendly rivalry or rooted in more intense competition, but that person also holds a key to your own growth as an individual by providing you with the stimulus you need to polish your act.

SEEKING APPLICANTS

Looking for your first job after graduation is a stressful process. It means hours spent working through your interviewing strategy, checking and rechecking your résumé, even rehearsing your posture and smile in front of the mirror. It's all about making a good impression; about letting them know you've got what they need. You're out there competing with a hundred other grads with the same GPA, the same part-time job experience, and the same extracurricular interests. A new suit and haircut aren't enough to set you apart from the crowd—you need to find a way to make the people in HR see the real you.

1. You have landed an interview at the company of your first choice. On the day of your interview, you are called down to a meeting room and you see that you're going to be interviewed by a team. What is the average age of the people on the panel of interviewers?

2. The interview is rigorous and thorough, with questions ranging from the simple "getting to know you" variety to ones that were clearly intended to rattle your cage. You manage to field every question thrown at you, but one in particular leaves a strong impression. What is that question?

3. Just when you are beginning to relax and feel the job is in the bag, one of the interviewers begins to point out your shortcomings

and weak points. What characteristics does your critic list among your faults?

4. That night, the phone rings. It's the HR manager calling with an offer! What do you say in response?

KEY TO "SEEKING APPLICANTS"

$\bigcirc$ ongratulations—you did it! Landing a job is cause for celebration, but it also means taking on a host of new responsibilities and challenges. It's one of the most important decisions you can make in determining the course of your life, almost like committing yourself to another person. In fact, there are many parallels between work and relationships; there are assignments of expectations and accountability, a need for teamwork and occasional sacrifice, and far-reaching consequences for success and failure. It's no wonder, then, that your responses to this scenario also reveal some of your hopes and expectations regarding romance and love.

1. The average age of your interviewers is the age of the person you see as your ideal partner. An interview is an opportunity not just to make, but also to form, an impression. The age of the imaginary decision makers at your ideal employer reflects your own preferences in the age of people you want to be involved with. A great majority of people see their ideal partner as roughly the same age or slightly older. If you said the panel comprised people much older than you, it may be that you have an eye for the "silver foxes."

2. The question that sticks most in your mind is actually something you would secretly like to ask your lover or spouse.

"Why did you choose this company?" We've all wanted to ask, "Why did you pick me?"

"Tell us about your hobbies and interests." Translation: "What do you do when I'm not around?"

"What makes you so interested in trying out this position?" That's a loaded question, but sometimes one that needs to be asked.

3. The faults that your interviewer listed are actually things your partner loves you for. A flaw that you acknowledge loses much of its negative force, and there's no shortcoming that can't be turned into a strength. The things that you have seen are wrong with you are things that you have already taken steps to compensate for.

"You're overconfident." That self-assuredness lends strength to others.

"Not proactive enough." You're easygoing, easy to live with, and easy to love.

"Too inexperienced." You bring a sense of freshness and boundless potential to a relationship.

4. Your reply to the offer of employment shows how you would re-act to a marriage proposal.

"Really? Are you serious! Great! I can't wait to get started." That's sure to start things off on the right foot, but you may want to play it a little closer to the vest until the deal is sealed. Too often people mistake eagerness for desperation.

"I'd like to think it over for a few days." That seems to be a sensible approach. There's no reason to jump in headfirst. After all, this is a very big commitment.

"Well, I've had a few other offers as well, so I'm going to take some time to weigh my options." Careful now, don't get too sure of yourself—it's likely they've had other applicants, too.

DREAM HOME

S ome people see their home merely as a shelter from the elements or a place to crash after a long day spent outside. But most attach deeper significance to the place they call home—feelings of safety, comfort, warmth, and love. However one may feel, the image of the home is defined by experiences and memories and gives shape to your dream of a perfect place to be. We've all had the experience of visiting someone's home for the first time and thinking, This is exactly how I imagined it would be. Homes are for hearts as well as bodies, and they tend to take on the characters of their occupants over time.

How would you describe your ideal home, the home you see yourself most comfortable in? Let's open the door and take a peek inside.

1. After years of hard work and saving, you are considering the purchase of your dream home. When you open the front door to begin the tour, there is a staircase immediately before you. Is it brightly illuminated or dimly lit?

2. The house has not been used for some time. Hallway, toilet, bathtub, dining room—which is most badly in need of cleaning? Which is the best kept?

3. As you walk from room to room, you notice the front door is still slightly open, and someone is peeping in through the crack. Who is that person?

KEY TO "DREAM HOME"

(A) ttaining your ideal home represents the fulfillment of your worldly aspirations and dreams in life. The image you had of your tour through your dream home is tied to your image of what the future holds in store for you.

1. The staircase symbolizes what lies ahead. Those who pictured a well-lit staircase have a clear set of goals and expectations for what is to come. Those who imagined a dark stairway have difficulty conceiving the direction their lives will take.

2. The area you perceived as dirtiest reveals an area in your life that you believe will give you the most problems in the future, while the cleanest area is what you hope will be the key to your happiness and success.

Hallway. A dirty hallway is a sign of anxiety about difficulties relating to other people, while a clean hallway signifies the hope of an unobstructed course through the world of interpersonal relationships.

Toilet. Those who imagined a clean toilet attach the most importance to financial security and success, while those who saw a dirty toilet fear money problems, debt, and bankruptcy in the future.

Bathtub. The bath is a symbol of health, and its level of cleanliness reflects one's hopes or concerns about physical well-being and sickness. A dirty tub equates with a fear of future illness and debilitation; a clean tub shows an attachment of great importance to the maintenance of good health.

Dining room. The dining room is the space devoted to the family as a whole. A dirty dining room is an omen of familial strife to come, while a clean dining room shows that the family is that person's highest priority.

3. Doors protect the home from the world outside. By peering through the door to watch as you visited your dream home, the person you named breached an important line of defense. That intruder is someone you perceive as a potential threat to your future happiness. It may even be someone you could never imagine intentionally causing you harm. It may be that person makes you uneasy because the people we love have the greatest power to hurt us. But then, the unconscious also has ways of sensing danger that the conscious mind chooses to ignore.